MACAO

Directed by: Josef von Sternberg
Screenplay by: Bernard C. Schoenfeld
and
Stanley Rubin

An Andrew Velez Book

FREDERICK UNGAR PUBLISHING CO.
New York

Published by arrangement with RKO General, Inc.

PUBLISHER'S NOTE:
This is the complete final screenplay for the RKO film.
The movie as released may differ from the screenplay
in some respects.

Printed in Great Britain
by Biddles of Guildford

ISBN 0-8044-6877-X

INTRODUCTION

The career of Josef von Sternberg was plagued by controversy. His work continues up to the present to be praised as that of a masterful cinematic magician, and dismissed as the product of a magnifier of bizarre trivialities. *Macao* was the second of two films he made for Howard Hughes. Production of the film was marked by disagreements between von Sternberg and Hughes that ended any possibility of the long relationship Hughes had promised they would have together. Ultimately, director Nicholas Ray (*Rebel Without a Cause*, etc.), was called in to re-shoot scenes, in particular a fist fight between Robert Mitchum and Brad Dexter. Action scenes of that sort were not von Sternberg's strength. He was sufficiently enraged to disown the film totally, although a viewing clearly shows it to be stamped as his stylistically.

Shooting on the film began in 1950. It was not released until 1952, a delay not uncommon for films with which Hughes became involved personally. *Jet Pilot*, the other feature von Sternberg directed for him, was filmed in 1950 and not released until 1957, after extensive re-shooting and editing. From the outset the two leading ladies in *Macao* were at odds with their director and objected to his arrogant manner. These embroilments contrasted with the response of Marlene Dietrich, who has written of him as "the man I most wanted to please."

The six films von Sternberg made with Dietrich, beginning with *The Blue Angel* (1930) through *The Devil Is a Woman* (1935), remain the enduring pinnacle of his career. Playing Pygmalion to her Galatea, he transformed her from a plump fräulein whom he discovered on the Berlin stage into a star and one of the screen's most enduring symbols of glamorous eroticism. Even as those films are evidence of his singular cinematic signature, so too *Macao* clearly evidences his characteristic skill with atmospheric touches and sexual byplay.

Von Sternberg completed only one more film. In 1953 he made *The Saga of Anatahan*, a remarkable dramatization of a true World War II incident about Japanese marines who refused to believe Japan had lost the war.

The plot of *Macao* is not unlike that of many other thrillers of the Forties and Fifties. *Saigon, Algiers, Casablanca*—they are all the same. What distinguishes them is atmosphere and decor and the chemistry among the players. In Jane Russell and Robert Mitchum, von Sternberg had leading actors who exuded sexuality. She is a caustic, not quite broken blossom poured into her gowns, and he is a sensitive tough guy who will dive into the sea to save a drowning coolie while others stand by indifferently. The script by Bernard C. Schoenfeld and Stanley Rubin based on a story by Bob Williams provided lively and cynical dialogue between them. The film is essentially a duel between Russell and Mitchum. Mitchum is persistent in pursuing her from the moment he spies her on board the ferry to Macao. In response to one of his passes she rebuffs him with an electric fan and he defends himself with a pillow. The room is filled with a storm of feathers—a perfect von Sternberg touch.

A chase scene near the climax of the picture has light sliding over Mitchum's face and his pursuer amidst hanging fishnets and bobbing junks of the harbor at night. This unreal atmosphere is reminiscent of von Sternberg's earlier *The Scarlet Empress* (1934) and *Underworld* (1927), and is yet further proof of how "colorful" a black-and-white film can be in the hands of a master. This is *film noir*: visually dynamic, sexy, filled with characters with shifting identities, sometimes confusing and, paradoxically, ingenuous.

Andrew Velez

CAST:

Nick Cochran	Robert Mitchum
Julie Benson	Jane Russell
Lawrence Trumble	William Bendix
Lieutenant Sebastian	Thomas Gomez
Margie	Gloria Grahame
Halloran	Brad Dexter
Martin Stewart	Edward Ashley
Itzumi	Philip Ahn
Kwan Sum Tang	Vladimir Sokoloff
Gimpy	Don Zelaya

CREDITS:

Screenplay	Bernard C. Schoenfeld and Stanley Rubin
Story	Bob Williams
Excutive Producer	Samuel Bischoff
Producer	Alex Gottlieb
Director	Josef von Sternberg
Songs	
''Ocean Breeze'' and	Jules Styne and
''You Kill Me''	Leo Robin
''One For My Baby''	Johnny Mercer (lyrics)
	Harold Arlen (music)
Music	Anthony Collins
Musical Director	C. Bakaleinikoff
Vocal Arrangements	Hugh Martin
Director of Photography	Harry J. Wild, A.S.C.
Art Directors	Albert S. D'Agostino
	Ralph Berger
Set Decorations	Darrell Silvera
	Harley Miller
Film Editors	Samuel E. Beetley, A.C.E.
	Robert Golden
Sound	Earl Wolcott
	Clem Portman
Gowns	Michael Woulfe
Makeup Artist	Mel Berns
Hair Stylist	Larry Germain

MACAO

FADE IN

Credit titles superimposed over a revolving globe. As it revolves, we move closer to the globe. We see the continent of Asia, then closer still, a map of the China coast, showing Hong Kong and the waters separating it from Macao.

DISSOLVE

EXTERIOR STERN OF BOAT—DAY
We see a wake of dirty water followed by scavengers—gulls and sharks.

FLAGS ON MASTHEAD
British and Portuguese Macao standards fluttering in the wind with screeching seagulls behind it.

FERRY BOAT
As it comes closer and we see its name painted on the bow.

CLOSEUP—A LAMBRECHT BAROMETER

1

Humidity and temperature are at 100-100. The needle points to a spot which reads: "Healthy for plants—unhealthy for human beings."

CHINESE MATE AT HELM
He is in tropical clothes. While steering, he opens a soda bottle, drains it, and aims the empty bottle at one of the screeching gulls.

A PILOT (PORTUGUESE)
He tries to cool himself by fanning with his pilot's cap. He talks Chinese to another mate, who phones orders below.

INTERIOR STOKER ROOM OF SHIP
Coolies at work. Their naked chests and shoulders are glistening with perspiration as they near the end of their work. They look at pictures of Chinese girls pasted or drawn in chalk on walls. One of them lets his girl-tattooed muscles quiver.

CHINESE MEMBER OF THE CREW
He throws out line to measure depth and speed. He looks up at top deck and sees—

JULIE BENTON
She is dressed in tropical clothes and a large hat. Her valise and an old traveling phonograph are on the deck. She constantly fans herself because of the intense heat and humidity. Life has obviously given Julie a severe beating, but she has retained a kind of defiance and self-respect. Many women like her might have become tramps—but part of Julie's strength lies in the fact that she has not.

NICK COCHRAN
Slumped in a chair, his hat over his face. He lifts up his hat, glances over at rail where Julie stands. He grins at what he sees.

JULIE

2

Straightening the seams of her stockings, a typical gesture. She, realizing she is being watched, looks over annoyed.

NICK
As he shrugs an apology and drops the hat back over his face.

EXTERIOR DECK OF THE SHIP—(SEPARATED FROM FIRST CLASS BY IRON BARS)
Against a railing, a group of coolies quarrel violently in Chinese. We see one of them pushed against the rail. We hear him cry out above the others. Then we see him lifted bodily and he falls over the rail.

GROUP OF EUROPEAN PASSENGERS
As they stand against the rail, talking in several languages. They see the coolie fall into the water. A woman begins to scream.
PASSENGER: *(shouting in Portuguese and English)* Man overboard!

A SIKH POLICEMAN
Assigned to the boat, he hears the shout of the passenger. He looks around casually, spits, and moves on unperturbed.

THE PILOT AND MATE
Mate at phone, unconcerned while pilot leans lazily over the rail to look.

HELMSMAN
He merely turns his head casually, then goes on steering without emotion.

NICK
He is in the act of dropping his shoes on the deck. Now he tosses aside his coat, climbs to the top of the rail, and dives into the choppy water.

JULIE
As she reacts with interest.

3

THE PILOT

PILOT: *(shouting)* Man overboard!

The Chinese mate phones excitedly to control room in Chinese.

CLOSE SHOT—ENGINE CONTROLS

Signals stop, then go into reverse.

THE MATE

He turns his steering wheel sharply.

A LIFEBELT WITH NAME OF SHIP

The lifebelt and rope are flung into the water.

THE CAPTAIN AND CREWMEN

As they rush to the rail of the turning boat.

NICK IN WATER

He swims to the Chinese, reaches him, loops his arm under the man's chin, and swims toward the lifebelt.

EXTERIOR TOP DECK—JULIE

She is watching the rescue intently. For a second, she forgets to fan herself, despite the great heat.

THE DECK OF THE BOAT

Body of the Chinese is pulled on board. Behind the body, Nick climbs on deck. He leans breathlessly for a second against the rail.

THE CAPTAIN

He turns the body of the Chinese over. We see the dagger in his back. A pool of blood quickly spreads.

JULIE

She continues to watch with interest, her eyes now focused on Nick.

NICK AND CAPTAIN

Nick glances down at the Chinese. Then he begins to wring sea water out of his shirt and trousers. While he is doing this, the captain wheels away from the dead body and turns on Nick savagely.

CAPTAIN: What's the idea of delaying my boat?! Haven't I trouble enough making the run from Hong Kong in three hours!

Nick continues calmly to wring out his shirt.

CAPTAIN: *(continued)* What makes you think I enjoy spinning this ferry like a top every time a fool decides to jump in this shark soup?

Nick moves to a pair of shoes lying on the deck. He begins to put them on.

CAPTAIN: *(continued) (now at the top of his voice)* Why did you have to butt in? He'd be at the bottom of the sea and nobody would have cared. Now I'll have my hands full!

Nick stoops, pushes the captain's foot off a white linen jacket lying on the deck.

NICK: *(with casual insolence)* Would it inconvenience you to take your foot off my freshly laundered jacket?

He dusts off his jacket, hunts in the pockets for a pack of cigarettes. He finds one, then looks in vain for matches.

CAPTAIN: I've run across your kind before—you're a troublemaker! Let's see your ticket.

Nick begins to fumble in his trousers pockets.

CAPTAIN: *(continued)* I thought so!

NICK: I'll be glad to jump back in and look for it.

CAPTAIN: *(roaring)* A passenger has to have a ticket. You can't get on without one—you can't get off without one—and you can't stay on this boat without one.

NICK: My ticket and my money were in my wallet—

CAPTAIN: And your wallet's on the bottom of the sea! Well—my friend—we'll fix that. When we get to Macao, I'll turn you over to the port authorities.

A stout middle-aged American, Trumble, comes into scene. He is the epitome of the extroverted salesman—voluble, cheerful, and good-natured.

TRUMBLE: Why don't you take it easy, Cap? It's too hot to get excited.

5

CAPTAIN: You wouldn't feel cool if a walking piece of driftwood messed up your schedule—and then had the gall to say he had no ticket and no money to pay his passage!

TRUMBLE: For a second I thought it was real serious. If it's only a ticket for this young fellow, I'll be more than glad to stake him to one. *(to Nick)* Any objections?

NICK: *(humorously)* Only as a formality.

TRUMBLE: *(handing money to captain)* This ought to cover it. *(taking a card out of wallet)* My name's Trumble. Lawrence C. Trumble. *(handing captain cigar)* Try one of these. You never smoked anything finer. *(offers one to Nick)* How about you, Mister—?

NICK: I'll take a light.

Trumble hands Nick the match. Nick lights the cigarette.

CAPTAIN: *(yelling to crewmen offstage)* Clean up this mess—swab down the deck—make it shipshape—*(with a furious glance at Nick, he exits)* Line up the third class—and let me look them over.

A group of crewmen appear. Two of them lift up the dead body just long enough for a third to clean away the blood. Then they let down the body of the Chinese onto the deck in the exact same position.

MOVING SHOT—NICK AND TRUMBLE

As they head toward the ship's bar.

TRUMBLE: You don't smoke cigars? Then you never heard of the China Sea Cigar Company in Manila. Old outfit—tops. I represent 'em. Also deal in coconut oil, pearl buttons, fertilizer—and nylon stockings. Means a pretty good income, plus expense account. Figure I can buy us a drink without going into debt.

NICK: Thanks.

They go into the bar.

INTERIOR THE BAR

It is really just a cubbyhole off deck. The bar is made of bamboo, and there are a couple of bamboo stools.

TRUMBLE: *(slaps counter)* Boy!

The Chinese bartender appears.

TRUMBLE: *(continued)* What'll you have?

6

NICK: That depends on our friend.

BARTENDER: Cognac, beer, and sarsaparilla.

NICK: *(dryly)* Make it sarsaparilla—and a chaser of cognac.

TRUMBLE: The same—and a pack of American cigarettes for Mr.— *(to Nick)* What'd you say the name was?

NICK: I didn't say. But it's Cochran—Nick Cochran.

The bartender brings cigarettes and two glasses, pours the drinks. Trumble pays, handing him a bill.

BARTENDER: Fifty dollars? I'll get the change from the purser.

He leaves. As Nick drinks, he looks up at the windows high on the deck side of the wall. Trumble looks up and follows his gaze.

WINDOW—FROM NICK'S EYELINE

Through the window, Julie's legs can be seen as she stands on deck.

TRUMBLE'S VOICE: Yeah, I noticed her, too. Pretty rundown—but good-looking. There's something about a white woman that looks good in this part of the world. The Chinese call 'em pink. We call 'em white—they say pink.

NICK'S VOICE: All depends which side of the fence you're on.

TRUMBLE'S VOICE: When a man sells stockings, he gets—interested in stockings. Take those up there, for instance, won't last a week. Coarse gauge—forty-five. Ought to have fifty-four. Wrong color, too.

NICK AND TRUMBLE

As Julie's legs move nearer the window.

NICK: *(laconically)* I just specialize in the shape.

The bartender returns with change—Trumble offers Nick a twenty-dollar bill.

TRUMBLE: *(as Nick hesitates)* You can pay me back in Macao.

NICK: *(finally accepting bill)* I wish I were as optimistic. Where you from?

TRUMBLE: Don't tell me I've lost my Brooklyn accent! Haven't been home in fourteen—no, more like sixteen years. Where do you get mail from?

NICK: I don't.

TRUMBLE: If you did—

7

NICK: New York, San Francisco, Dallas, Kansas City—unless they're all married by now. *(looking at Trumble's ring)* The real McCoy?

TRUMBLE: *(dryly)* Fake—gotta put up a front in my work.

NICK: How'd *you* get stuck in this part of the world?

TRUMBLE: Had a funny boss back home—kind of sensitive. Didn't like people working for him who juggled accounts.

NICK: Nobody ever stays out here for more than a couple of months without a reason. *(looking up at Julie's legs—reflectively)* I wonder what hers is.

TRUMBLE: *(quietly)* What's yours?

NICK: *(evasively—as he finishes drink)* I better get these clothes off before I start steaming.

TRUMBLE: See you later.

Nick goes off. Trumble looks after him. He relights his cigar, then starts out to the deck.

DISSOLVE

EXTERIOR DECK—JULIE
She stands at the rail, holding onto her big hat. There is a loneliness about the way she stands here, looking out over the water. Trumble comes in carrying a small traveling salesman's case, not much larger than a briefcase, leans on rail for a moment before he speaks.

TRUMBLE: We'll be in soon—only about fifteen minutes late.

Julie looks at him.

TRUMBLE: *(continued)* First trip to Macao?

JULIE: Yes—and from what I hear, once is once too much.

TRUMBLE: That's what I hear. *(sighs)* But when you're in business like I am, you got to go where they send you. Why are *you* making the trip?

JULIE: *(suspiciously)* Got any small questions?

TRUMBLE: *(with a grin)* Like the wife tells me, I talk too much—don't I?

JULIE: That's okay. I just don't warm up to questions—when I don't know the answers myself.

8

TRUMBLE: Saw you when you got on at Hong Kong. I'd like to introduce myself—the name's Trumble. Lawrence C. Trumble, dealer in coconut oil, pearl buttons, fertilizers—nylon hose.

JULIE: No sale on your other lines, Mr. Trumble—*(looking at the run in her stocking)* Did I hear you mention nylons?

TRUMBLE: *(eyeing her legs)* Size nine?

JULIE: Eight and a half. *(as he opens his case)* But don't work so fast. How much are they?

TRUMBLE: For free. *(as she looks at him sharply)* No strings attached.

JULIE: *(smiling)* The price is right.

Trumble draws out three pairs of nylons and hands them to her. She looks questioningly at the idea of three free pairs.

TRUMBLE: Our special for today.

She walks over to a bench hooked to the wall and begins to slip off her shoes, first putting the extra pairs in her purse.

JULIE: I'll never believe another traveling salesman story.

She takes off her old stockings and rolls them up.

JULIE: *(continued)* What are they going to do to the guy who went swimming?

TRUMBLE: Well, they won't receive him with a brass band. Fine thing he did—riskin' his life like that.

JULIE: Wouldn't be a bad idea to have a guy like that around when *I* get ready to jump.

TRUMBLE: You could do worse—seems to be a nice fella.

JULIE: I'm no good on men. Made a lot of mistakes that way.

She rolls up her stockings, throws them on the deck. The wind moves them along until they stop at Nick's feet as he comes up the stairs. He has on a dry suit. He looks over, sees Julie offstage.

JULIE
She is pulling the second stocking up over her knee as she senses that someone is looking at her. She glances up.

JULIE: Enjoying the view?

NICK
As he grins and comes over to them.

NICK: Well, it's not the Taj Mahal or the Hanging Gardens of Babylon, but it'll do.

JULIE: Grandma, did anyone ever tell you what big blue eyes you have?

She pulls her skirt down, gets up.

TRUMBLE: Nick, I want you to meet an old friend of mine—Miss . . .

JULIE: Your old friend's name is Julie Benton. Thanks again, Mr. Trumble.

She goes off down the same stairs that Nick took up. Trumble and Nick watch her.

TRUMBLE: Looks like you made a big hit.

NICK: Yeah—it's my fatal charm. Never misses—except with women.

As he toys with Julie's discarded stockings, we . . .

DISSOLVE

EXTERIOR CUSTOMS DOCK—DAY

As the passengers stream down the gangplank. Native guides, hotel agents, rickshas and coolies, etc., are in evidence. The captain of the boat stands at the foot of the gangplank, checking the passengers off with another officer. Julie gets off, followed by another passenger, then Nick and Trumble.

NICK: Ah, my friend the captain! Must have been a dull trip for you this time—only one murder!

The captain glares after him, then camera moves with him as he goes over to Police Lieutenant Sebastian, who is eyeing the arriving passengers keenly. He is a handsome, middle-aged Portuguese, debonair and corruptible.

CAPTAIN: Lieutenant Sebastian . . .

SEBASTIAN: *(turning)* Yes, Captain . . .

CAPTAIN: *(pointing)* The man who pulled the body out.

Sebastian looks with definite interest.

NICK AND TRUMBLE

As he puts a cigarette in his mouth and hunts for a match. With a grin, Trumble hands him a match and walks off. Nick looks for a

10

place to strike the match. Near him on a wall is a sign proclaiming "Smoking Forbidden" in several languages. Nick strikes his match across the sign, becomes aware someone is watching him. He looks as he lights his cigarette.

SEBASTIAN
Eyeing Nick with suspicion. Then he smiles as he sees that Nick is aware of him.

NICK
He smiles back, indicating his cigarette.

TRUMBLE AND JULIE
As they pass a group of beggars, and Trumble throws them a handful of coins. They hurry to take their places in line at the customs, and Nick falls in behind them.

FULL SHOT—AT CUSTOMS TABLE
Revealing an Oriental photographer with an ancient camera is snapping flashgun pictures of each passenger lining up for inspection at the desk. Here the officials check passports, examine luggage, etc.
PHOTOGRAPHER: *(handing out tickets after taking pictures)* Mail in card with one dollar—get fine picture. Mail in two dollar—get two fine picture.

JULIE, TRUMBLE, AND NICK
As they wait in line.
TRUMBLE: This is one of those days when the customs'll make us sweat.
JULIE: Every time you enter a port around these parts, they go through your bags like they had nothing else to do.
NICK: They haven't. *(as a joke)* Smuggling anything in?
JULIE: The way I hear it, you smuggle things *out* of here—not *in.*

CUSTOMS OFFICIAL AND JULIE

11

He has heard her remark. Resenting it, he takes her valise and dumps the contents on the dirty floor.

OFFICIAL: Your passport, please.

As Julie gets it out of her purse and presents it, the photographer flash-bulbs a picture of Julie, hands her a card.

NICK AND TRUMBLE

As Nick leans over to talk low to Trumble.

NICK: What happens when he finds out *my* passport was in my wallet?

TRUMBLE: You sure do everything the hard way.

JULIE AND OFFICIAL

As he returns passport after stamping it.

OFFICIAL: Anything to declare, senhora?

JULIE: Yes. I declare—I'd like to get to a hotel and cool off.

JULIE'S VALISE

As the official bends down and starts to go through the contents. There's an extra dress, a kimono, a few toilet articles, not much else.

OFFICIAL'S VOICE: How much money are you bringing with you?

JULIE'S VOICE: Twenty-nine dollars—Mex. And a handful of Hong Kong paper.

JULIE AND OFFICIAL

As he dumps her clothes back into the valise.

OFFICIAL: How long do you plan to be here?

JULIE: Your guess is as good as mine.

OFFICIAL: How long were you in Hong Kong?

JULIE: Three or four weeks.

OFFICIAL: What were you doing there?

JULIE: You don't really want me to tell you, do you?

OFFICIAL: Where were you before you came to Hong Kong?

JULIE: Saigon.

OFFICIAL: How long were you in Saigon?

JULIE: *(in a flash of temper)* Say, what's going on here? First you throw my things around, then you keep asking me a lot of personal questions! Maybe *you* don't mind baking in this oven, but I do.

OFFICIAL: *(unperturbed)* And this box contains?

JULIE: What's left of my past.

OFFICIAL: *(calmly)* The key, please.

Julie fumbles through her pocketbook for her key and opens the phonograph. The official takes a record and puts it on. He hears Julie's voice with an orchestra. Everything becomes hushed for a moment while passengers and officials listen to Julie singing. Nick reacts with surprise to Trumble.

OFFICIAL: *(continued)* Why didn't you say you are a singer, senhora?

JULIE: You never asked me.

The official gestures to Trumble, who steps up.

OFFICIAL: Your passport, please.

The photographer gives his spiel and snaps Trumble's picture as Trumble poses for him after handing over passport. He pockets the card the photographer hands him.

TRUMBLE: *(opening valise)* That's me—Lawrence C. Trumble. Manila. Dealer in coconut oil, pearl buttons, fertilizer, nylon hose—and cigars.

OFFICIAL: Any contraband?

TRUMBLE: *(reaching into case)* Try some. Best in the world.

The official accepts the handful of cigars, smells them, puts the cigars in his pocket.

OFFICIAL: *(closing Trumble's valise)* Thank you, senhor. You have currency?

TRUMBLE: Five hundred greenbacks printed in the U.S.A. *(laughing)* Expect to have a lot more when I leave—if the dice get as hot as the weather.

OFFICIAL: *(stamping his passport—friendly)* In Macao everything is a gamble. *(in Portuguese)* Good luck.

Julie impatiently stops her record and closes the box as Nick moves up in line with his valise.

OFFICIAL: *(opening Nick's valise)* Your passport, senhor.

He waits impatiently while the photographer snaps Nick's picture and hands him a card, which Nick promptly throws away.

13

OFFICIAL: *(continued) (sharply)* Your passport, senhor.
NICK: You look like a man who admires frankness so I'll tell you the truth—I lost it.

SEBASTIAN
As he smiles knowingly at Nick's statement.

NICK AND OFFICIAL
OFFICIAL: Kindly report to the police at once.
He nods toward Lieutenant Sebastian offstage, then clicks Nick's valise shut.

SEBASTIAN
As Julie moves past him, carrying her phonograph and valise, on her way to the rickshas. When she passes, Sebastian eyes her.
JULIE: *(to ricksha driver)* Hotel Portugueza.
She gets into ricksha and is driven away as Nick comes into scene. Silently Sebastian and Nick look at Julie offstage.

JULIE IN RICKSHA—(PROCESS)
As Julie looks back over her shoulder at Nick.

NICK AND SEBASTIAN
Sebastian's eyes are still following Julie in the ricksha.
NICK: Don't let me drag you away from the line of duty. But I was told to report to you.
SEBASTIAN: *(turning to him)* I am Lieutenant Felizardo José Espirito Sebastian. At your service.
NICK: My passport's at the bottom of your beautiful harbor.
SEBASTIAN: *(pleasantly)* Ah yes, I hard of that curious episode, senhor.
NICK: What happens now—do I get deported or thrown in the clink?
SEBASTIAN: Neither, senhor—this is a Portuguese colony—always friendly and hospitable. Have you any other identification?
NICK: A birthmark that used to get big laughs when I was a baby.
SEBASTIAN: This is a serious matter, senhor.

14

Nick clicks open his valise and produces an envelope from which he takes a paper and hands it to Sebastian.
NICK: This took me three years, five months, and twenty-six days to get.

TRUMBLE
He is listening with interest to this conversation.

NICK AND SEBASTIAN
SEBASTIAN: *(as he reads paper)* Ah yes—you served as a lieutenant in the Signal Corps of the United States. Unfortunately, senhor, this finely engraved document does not grant you the privilege of traveling free as a bird throughout the Orient.
NICK: That doesn't sound good, does it?
SEBASTIAN: I suggest you contact your consulate in Hong Kong. How long did you intend to remain in our city?
NICK: That depends.
SEBASTIAN: On what?
NICK: Lady Luck.
SEBASTIAN: I wish you well, senhor. It is our fond hope that all visitors to Macao should feel as untroubled here as Adam did in the Garden of Eden.
NICK: Untroubled? That's not the way I heard it.
Nick walks away and joins Trumble.
NICK: *(continued) (low, as he goes)* I don't get this red-carpet treatment, do you?
TRUMBLE: It's your big blue eyes.
Camera moves with Sebastian as he strolls up to the Oriental photographer. The photographer slips his bony fingers into a bag and draws out a batch of photographs which he slips to Sebastian.

GROUP SHOT—NICK, TRUMBLE, AND RICKSHA DRIVERS
The ricksha drivers are all vying for favor. In pidgin English they are chanting, "Classy hotel take you—good hotel—take you," etc. At this moment a bus chugs up and a toothless, ancient Chinese driver shuffles out. Undoubtedly, he has arrived a few

minutes late. Around his neck he wears a sign "Hotel Portu-gueza."

DRIVER: *(disinterestedly)* Hotel Portugueza?

NICK: *(to Trumble)* Where did our friend go?

TRUMBLE: To the Portugueza. *(to the driver)* Between you and me, how's the food at your place?

DRIVER: *(grinning)* Terrible.

TRUMBLE: Are the rooms clean?

DRIVER: *(a wider grin)* Feelthy.

TRUMBLE: How's the service?

DRIVER: *(shrugging)* What service?

NICK: Sounds ideal.

He enters bus.

TRUMBLE: *(to driver)* Do you have to reserve rooms in advance?

DRIVER: *(helping Trumble into bus)* Only if you wish to be charged double.

TRUMBLE: Not me. I'm saving it for the gambling houses. Where are they?

DRIVER: *(getting in)* Where *aren't* they, senhor? *(vehemently)* I wish they would burn them all to the ground—*(with a sigh)*—as soon as I make one big killing.

The bus moves off.

SEBASTIAN

As he stands flipping the photographs against his fingers, his eyes following the bus. Then he walks to the car which has been waiting for him. The chauffeur leaps out, opens the door, gets into the car, and it moves off.

DISSOLVE

INTERIOR BUS—(PROCESS)—DAY

Trumble and Nick are looking at the many sights.

DRIVER: This is the Rua da Felicidade. Mucho fun—win plenty money—fan-tan—dice—big gambling. *(pointing)* This biggest gambling-house—run by American gentleman.

TRUMBLE: Yeah? What's his name?

16

DRIVER: Mr. Vincent Halloran. Very important man. Big boss.
NICK: What's he boss of?
DRIVER: Most of Macao ...
They look out.

MOVING SHOT—THE QUICK REWARD
Camera stops on electric sign (it is still afternoon and the sign is not lighted) which reads THE QUICK REWARD. *Camera continues down and into lower gambling hall.*

INTERIOR QUICK REWARD—LOWER FLOOR
At a fan-tan table a Chinese of the shopkeeper class is arguing vehemently with the croupier. There are only a few players at this time of the day and they are listening to the argument.
Shooting up to balcony of gambling house. Halloran leans over to watch the disturbance. He is a heavy-set, good-looking American, whose eyes seem to be made of ice.
HALLORAN: Ching—what's he beefing about?

SHOOTING DOWN INTO GAMBLING PIT
CROUPIER: Mr. Halloran, he claims that we cheated. He put ten Mex. on number three and says my rake interfered with his dice.

BALCONY RAIL
HALLORAN: *(shouting down)* Pay him off and throw him out.

GAMBLING ROOM DOWNSTAIRS
The croupier pays off the Chinese and signals the bouncers, who pounce on the Chinese and give him the bum's rush to the street door.

EXTERIOR STREET
The Chinese is dumped on the sidewalk. His silver scatters and he proceeds from his prone position to recoup it. Sebastian's car grinds to a stop. Sebastian, emerging, takes in the situation, picks up some of the silver, enters gambling house.

17

UPPER GALLERY

Waiters are preparing for the night, placing cashew nuts, water-melon seeds, and other delicacies for the wealthy, who do not mingle with hoi polloi *and who look down through four pits to the gambling tables below, where they lower their bids in baskets. Halloran moves toward his office door and opens it.*

INTERIOR HALLORAN'S OFFICE

His office is furnished in a mixture of East and West. On a desk lies a narrow basket in which are glittering pieces of jewelry as well as greenbacks and checks. In the room is Margie, a most attractive wench in her middle twenties.

She looks up as Halloran comes in. He moves to his desk and sits down, preoccupied. Margie moves close to him, bends to kiss his cheek. Without being too obvious, he draws his cheek away. She picks up a diamond brooch from the desk, is about to pin it to her when he takes it away.

HALLORAN: Diamonds would only cheapen you.

MARGIE: Sure—but what a way to be cheapened.

INTERIOR LOWER FLOOR

Close moving shot—basket, as it rises to the upper gallery. Itzumi, a cold hoodlum of the Orient, stands by a pit waiting. He takes a bracelet out of the basket and moves toward Halloran's office.

INTERIOR HALLORAN'S OFFICE

Halloran is examining the week's profits as Itzumi enters. Margie is lighting a cigarette.

ITZUMI: *(showing bracelet)* Ling Tan the merchant wants chips for this. He claims it is worth two thousand.

HALLORAN: *(after examining the bracelet carefully)* Who says it isn't? Offer him seven hundred. *(as Itzumi turns)* Did your cousin arrive on the noon ferry?

ITZUMI: If he had, he would be here by now.

HALLORAN: It shouldn't take five days to sell a hundred-thousand-dollar necklace in Hong Kong and come back—if he's coming back.

18

ITZUMI: He has always returned before.
HALLORAN: That's what I mean.
They turn as Sebastian hurries in.
SEBASTIAN: *(preening)* As I anticipated, my connections in Hong Kong were absolutely right! No uniform—no badge—no official credentials—but I spotted him—*(snapping fingers)*—like that!
HALLORAN: Stop taking bows and let's see what he looks like.
Sebastian hurries over to the desk with the photographs.
SEBASTIAN: *(as he makes two piles)* These passengers we already know. But these three are newcomers.
HALLORAN: *(during following action)* Doesn't a murder charge ever get outlawed?
Halloran discards the one pile, picks up one of the three pictures in the other pile. Margie picks up one of the two remaining pictures.
SEBASTIAN: He will not be as easy as the last one.

INSERT   TRUMBLE'S PHOTOGRAPH
In Halloran's hand.
HALLORAN'S VOICE: He looks easy enough.

SEBASTIAN AND HALLORAN
SEBASTIAN: *(impatiently)* No, no—that is just a salesman—Senhor Trumble from Manila. *(handing him Nick's picture)* This is the New York detective!

INSERT   NICK'S PHOTOGRAPH
HALLORAN'S VOICE: As soon as a man represents the law, he gets a look on his face that he can't lose—like a large wart.

GROUP SHOT
HALLORAN: *(still looking at Nick's face)* Where is he now—at headquarters?
SEBASTIAN: No, senhor. Nor do I think he will ever visit the police. This man—he is going under the name of Nick Cochran—is very clever. Right now he is at the Hotel Portugueza, pretending to be without money or passport.

HALLORAN: Did you talk to him at all?

SEBASTIAN: Oh—I welcomed him in my most charming manner. He insisted on concealing his identity, so I played his little game. Obviously he has some plan to take you back to New York—illegally. This, senhor, will happen over your dead body.

HALLORAN: *(sardonically)* That's what I like about you, Sebastian— your unselfishness.

Margie is holding Julie's picture.

MARGIE: I often wonder what men see in women—thank goodness! *Halloran takes the picture out of her hand.*

INSERT   JULIE'S PICTURE

HALLORAN'S VOICE: How does she appeal to you, Sebastian?

GROUP SHOT

SEBASTIAN: Unfortunately I am a married man—and try not to think of such things.

MARGIE: *(indicating Halloran)* Unfortunately he's *not.*

She exits as Itzumi holds the door open politely for her.

HALLORAN: *(indicating Julie's photograph)* Think she's hooked up with him?

SEBASTIAN: I never considered the possibility.

HALLORAN: Where's she staying?

SEBASTIAN: At his hotel.

HALLORAN: *(with wry disgust)* Felizardo, some day you must explain to me how you ever became a police lieutenant.

SEBASTIAN: I have often wondered myself.

HALLORAN: Did they seem to know each other?

SEBASTIAN: They hardly spoke a word at the dock.

HALLORAN: What does she say she's here for?

SEBASTIAN: Besides her obvious talents, she sings . . .

Halloran continues to look at Julie's picture.

DISSOLVE

INTERIOR JULIE'S ROOM—AFTERNOON

20

CLOSE SHOT—PHONOGRAPH
We hear Julie's voice singing on a record. Camera pulls back to reveal Julie in a cheap kimono, finishing the remnants of a Chinese supper. With her chopsticks she pushes away the last bit of chopped meat and bean sprouts. She listens to her own voice on the record, then restlessly she gets up, goes over to the window, looks out.

DOCKS AND HARBOR—FROM JULIE'S EYELINE
The slanting roofs . . . the zigzag cubistic patterns . . . the calm waters, the junks. Suddenly Julie's voice on the phonograph grows dissonant.

JULIE
Drearily she turns away from the window, comes to the phonograph and shuts it off. Suddenly a sharp yell of Nick's voice is heard in the corridor. Julie's face brightens. She hurries to the door, opens it.

HOTEL CORRIDOR
As Julie comes out.
NICK'S VOICE: *(shouting)* Hey, what do I have to do to get some service around here?
Julie looks down the corridor.

NICK FROM JULIE'S EYELINE
He is leaning over the balustrade, shouting down to the lobby. He is stripped to the waist, with a handkerchief tied around his sweating forehead. Suddenly he sees Julie.

JULIE
She is conscious of being caught in the act of looking at him. Flustered, she draws her kimono closer around her and returns into her room.

NICK

21

He places two fingers in his mouth and emits a sharp, piercing whistle. At this moment Trumble appears on the landing, coming downstairs.

TRUMBLE: *(good-naturedly)* Thought the hotel was on fire.

NICK: *(wiping brow)* Isn't it?

TRUMBLE: *(grinning at Nick's bareness)* That's not a bad idea—dressing formal.

He continues down the stairs.

LOBBY

As the desk clerk hurries in and looks up at Nick.

NICK: I've got some clothes to be cleaned. How long will it take?

CLERK: One hour, senhor. I will send someone up for them.

NICK: How long will that take?

CLERK: One hour, senhor.

NICK: Let's save some time.

Nick throws the wet suit and shirt with unerring aim. The clerk tries to catch it. The ball of linen hurtles onto the clerk's face as Trumble comes to the bottom of the stairs.

TRUMBLE: *(grinning up at Nick—in the manner of a barker)* The gentleman wins a kewpie doll!

Nick waves to Trumble and walks back down the hall.

CLERK: Ah—Senhor Trumble—

TRUMBLE: Where can I get a shave around here?

CLERK: We have the finest barber in the Orient, senhor. Right this way.

Trumble follows clerk to the doorway of the barber shop in lobby.

INTERIOR BARBER SHOP

It is not a shop at all, but merely one high bamboo chair and a stand on which are razors and paraphernalia. The barber is a very decorative Japanese girl. Trumble hands the clerk a cigar and at the same time offers one to the Japanese girl, who takes it. Trumble removes his coat, unloosens his collar, sits in the chair.

TRUMBLE: *(to clerk, during above)* I didn't see any phone in my room. How do you call Hong Kong?

CLERK: Senhor, there is not only no telephone in your room, but we have never had a telephone connection with Hong Kong. If you wish to cable, the phone at my desk is at your disposal.
TRUMBLE: Thanks.

The girl barber has lathered up by now and starts to work on him.
TRUMBLE: *(continued)* Once over very lightly, Madame Butterfly—I've got a skin like a baby's bottom.

He relaxes comfortably.

JULIE'S ROOM
The ceiling fan does not seem to do much good. Julie opens the shutters to the balcony, steps out.

EXTERIOR BALCONY (PROCESS)
As Julie appears. She breathes deeply, looks out.

MACAO HARBOR AND DOCKS
We see the panorama stretching before us.

JULIE
Just then there is the sound of shutters opening next door. She glances in that direction.
Nick comes out of his room, a casual push closing the door behind him. Julie looks at him as he pulls up the blind.
JULIE: *(obviously suffering from the heat)* Hi.
NICK: I know just how you feel.
JULIE: *(with a faint smile)* How long do you suppose it takes before dry rot sets in?
NICK: Depends on why you're here. *(offering an open pack)* Cigarette?
JULIE: Smoking's not one of my vices.
NICK: Got a match?
JULIE: I'll get you one.
She goes into her room.

INTERIOR JULIE'S ROOM

23

As she comes in to table near door. Nick comes in behind her, but she is not aware of it. She picks up pack of matches, turns.

NICK: *(taking matches from her)* Thanks. *(as he lights cigarette)* Am I keeping you from anything?

JULIE: My bath.

NICK: The harbor's cooler—and there's room for both of us.

JULIE: Sorry. Have to look for work this afternoon.

NICK: How about tonight?

JULIE: I hope I'll be working by then.

NICK: Well, that kills today. How early in the morning can we get together?

Suddenly there is a knock on Julie's door.

JULIE: *(puzzled)* Who could that be?

NICK: The irate husband, if memory serves me.

JULIE: I'm not married, never been married, don't expect to be married. *(as knock is heard again)* Come in.

They watch as Sebastian enters offstage.

NICK: Adam in the Garden of Eden.

Grinning, he leaves by the balcony. With a click of his heels and a salute. Sebastian announces himself.

SEBASTIAN: I am Lieutenant Felizardo José Espirito Sebastian, in charge of the Fifth Police District, which includes this hotel. *(as he walks in)* May I come in?

JULIE: Don't you mean—barge in?

SEBASTIAN: I should like to explain that I am not here in my official capacity.

JULIE: All the more reason why you should leave.

SEBASTIAN: In a moment, senhora. But first I hope to be of no small service to you.

JULIE: *(disbelieving)* I've heard that one before.

SEBASTIAN: You misunderstand.

JULIE: Okay. What's on your mind?

SEBASTIAN: I was standing on the dock when I heard your voice on that record, senhora. "Well, Felizardo," I said to myself. "There is a young lady whose voice can add to the beauty of Macao." I am a worshipper of—

24

At this point his monologue is interrupted by a sound outside on the balcony, which seems to combine the clattering of shutters with some inarticulate oaths. He stops, irritated, and glances toward the open balcony window.

EXTERIOR BALCONY OUTSIDE NICK'S ROOM
Nick is trying desperately to get into his room, but he is locked out.

INTERIOR JULIE'S ROOM
Sebastian turns back to her.
SEBASTIAN: So being a man with a practical side to my nature I hurried—
At this moment Nick casually walks through the room. Sebastian stops talking.
NICK: *(to Sebastian)* Nice to see you again, Lieutenant.
He exits by Julie's door.
SEBASTIAN: And so I hurried to a friend of mine—Senhor Vincent Halloran, owner of the largest gambling establishment in town. "Vincent," I said, "our friendship is over unless you give this girl a chance." Naturally, he could not dare risk losing my friendship.
JULIE: Is all that lingo trying to hide the fact that you've got me a job?
SEBASTIAN: Precisely.
JULIE: Why didn't you come right out with it?
SEBASTIAN: Your pardon, please. When can you be at his office?
JULIE: As soon as you leave so I can get dressed.
SEBASTIAN: *(bowing, in Portuguese)* Good-bye, Miss Benton. It has been a pleasure to welcome a young lady graced with such beauty of face and soul.
JULIE: *(not understanding a single word)* Same here, officer.
Sebastian takes her hand, kisses it, leaves. Julie looks after him, then with renewed energy hurries to her closet and takes out her best dress.

HOTEL CORRIDOR

*Sebastian stands a moment outside, smiles shrewdly, then goes to
Nick's door. He listens, then continues on his way.*

DISSOLVE

EXTERIOR QUICK REWARD—AFTERNOON
*A ricksha pulls up and Julie gets out. She searches in her purse for
the ricksha fee, hands the coolie some coins. The coolie begins to
gesticulate wildly and shouts epithets in Cantonese.*
JULIE: You no foolee me. I give you plenty tavos! I give you too
much and you wantchee more! Beat it!
*Hopping up and down as though he were doing a war dance, the
ricksha driver reaches toward Julie's purse. Julie looks around
quickly.*

TRAFFIC COP—FROM JULIE'S EYELINE
*He is a great, bushy-bearded brute of a Sikh, directing traffic at
the corner.*
JULIE'S VOICE: Hey!
*Traffic cop reacts. Traffic is forgotten. He parts his beard, shows
his pearly white teeth and takes a step forward, makes a com-
manding gesture toward the coolie.*

JULIE AND COOLIE
JULIE: Cop put you in clinker—chop-chop.
*The coolie looks in the direction of the cop, sees that all is not well,
and taking up his ricksha, breaks into a trot.*

JULIE
*She adjusts her stockings, prior to entering the Quick Reward. As
she does so, a weird tapping is heard close by. Then a long, bony
hand reaches out a tin cup. Camera angles to include Kwan Sum
Tang, a blind Chinese beggar. His thin face is wise and kindly.*
KWAN SUM TANG: *(in halting English)* Where—am I?
JULIE: The Quick Reward.
She drops a coin into his cup.

26

KWAN SUM TANG: There is an invisible reward and a visible reward—there is a late reward and a quick reward.
He moves on as Julie enters gambling house.

INTERIOR QUICK REWARD
The place is beginning to fill up. Already a few of the wealthy clientele have arrived, separating themselves from the lower class by sitting up on the gallery floor. The croupier at the fan-tan table is Margie. She reacts as she sees Julie enter.

JULIE
She glances around. She is a stimulant even to these impassive Chinese gamblers. She realizes she is being stared at. Camera moves with her as she spots the only white woman on the floor and comes to Margie, who is busy at the table, her back to Julie.
JULIE: Excuse me.
MARGIE: *(turning)* Yes . . .
JULIE: Where do I find Mr. Halloran—he sent for me.
MARGIE: Of course. What do *you* do—sing or dance?
JULIE: Why?
MARGIE: The last one danced. *(pointing)* You'll find him in his office—up those stairs.
JULIE: Thanks.
She exits as we hold on Margie looking after her.
MARGIE: *(to bland Chinaman)* What does Confucius say about this sort of thing?

JULIE
As she goes up the winding stairs, the center of attraction.

UPPER FLOOR GALLERY
As Julie arrives. The wealthy Chinese and the tourists glance at her and several of the men are so attracted that they even forget to place their bets in the baskets. Camera moves with her as she walks to the door and knocks. The door is opened by Itzumi.
JULIE: Mr. Halloran in?

27

Itzumi does not answer, but opens the door wider, then closes it after her.

INTERIOR HALLORAN'S OFFICE
Halloran is sitting behind his desk. He looks up as Julie enters.
JULIE: Hello. That policeman friend of yours said you might have a job for me.
HALLORAN: I might. Miss Benton, isn't it?
Julie nods and sits. Halloran offers her a cigarette.
JULIE: No, thanks.
HALLORAN: *(putting her at her ease)* I've heard that all roads lead to Macao. But why did *you* want to come here?
JULIE: *(evasively)* I was left a legacy and I wanted to see the world.
HALLORAN: *(looking at her steadily)* You must meet a great number of people on your travels. *(sliding Nick's photograph across the desk to her)* This fellow, for instance?

INSERT   NICK'S PHOTOGRAPH
As Julie's fingers hold it.
JULIE'S VOICE: Sure.

HALLORAN AND JULIE
HALLORAN: Who is he?
JULIE: My grandfather. My mother won't let me go anywhere without a chaperon.
HALLORAN: *(with a pleasant smile)* I thought maybe he was part of your—seeing the world.
JULIE: I just met him on the boat.
Halloran looks at her searchingly.
HALLORAN: And now that your—legacy has almost been used up, you need a job.
JULIE: *(defensively)* This wasn't my idea, Mr. Halloran. You sent for me.
HALLORAN: We'll get along better if you take that chip off your shoulder. It won't get you anywhere here.
JULIE: *(her good nature returning)* It never got me anywhere—any place—

HALLORAN: Where have you sung?

JULIE: *(evasively)* Everywhere.

HALLORAN: I mean—recently?

JULIE: In Hong Kong until the boss got ideas.

HALLORAN: I can easily see why. Shall we say a hundred a week—American money?

JULIE: I'd sing better for a hundred and fifty.

HALLORAN: My patrons come here to gamble. I'll pay you a hundred. Think it over.

JULIE: I just did. When do I go on?

For answer, Halloran leaves the desk, goes to the door and opens it.

HALLORAN: *(to Itzumi)* Call Gimpy.

He closes the door again and comes back to the desk.

HALLORAN: *(continued)* I imagine you could stand a new wardrobe—how about two weeks' salary in advance?

JULIE: For once I won't say "no."

HALLORAN: *(taking bills out of a wallet and counting them)* This fellow you met on the boat—what does he do for a living?

JULIE: *(taking the money—shrewdly)* Why don't you ask him?

At this moment the door opens and Gimpy comes in. He is a native man of many races, who can play Bach and jazz with equal facility. His clubfoot proclaims his name.

HALLORAN: Gimpy, Miss Benton is going to sing here.

GIMPY: That is fine, Miss Benton.

JULIE: Glad to meet you, Mr.—

HALLORAN: *(as she hesitates)* He doesn't mind. Everyone calls him Gimpy. Don't they—Gimpy?

GIMPY: *(with a wry smile)* Everyone—Mr. Halloran.

HALLORAN: Find something for her to wear tonight. *(to Julie)* See you later.

JULIE: Thanks, Mr. Halloran.

HALLORAN: Try calling me Vince.

JULIE: *(meaningly)* Thanks—boss.

A look passes between them. Then Julie and Gimpy go out.

EXTERIOR UPPER GALLERY

29

As Julie and Gimpy come out. Itzumi stands at the door.
NICK'S VOICE: Got a match, lady?
*Julie turns. She almost conceals the pleasure at seeing him again,
but not quite. Nick comes into scene. He is dressed neatly, even
though the suit has seen better days.*
JUILE: Hi. What are you doing here?

INTERIOR HALLORAN'S ROOM
Halloran has the door ajar. In background he sees Nick.
NICK'S VOICE: Looking around.
He closes the door.

EXTERIOR UPPER GALLERY

JULIE, NICK, AND GIMPY
NICK: Don't tell me you landed a job?
JULIE: *(happily)* Meet my piano player, Mr.—
GIMPY: Gimpy.
NICK: My name's Cochran. Glad to meet you. *(turning to Julie—
warmly)* Nice going. *(confidentially)* Tell me—what sort of character
is this Halloran?
JULIE: *(lowering her voice)* He's a collector—of snapshots.
NICK: Snapshots?
JULIE: *(confidentially)* You know those photos of us they took on the
dock? They're on his desk.
NICK: Why?
JULIE: I don't know—but he was sure pumping me about you.
NICK: What did you tell him?
JULIE: All I knew—nothing. *(as she moves off with Gimpy)* Good
luck.

INTERIOR HALLORAN'S OFFICE
*Halloran takes a gun from his pocket, puts it in a convenient
drawer. He looks at Itzumi and nods for him to open the door. As
Itzumi does so, Nick is caught in the act of raising his knuckles to
rap.*

HALLORAN: *(cheerfully)* Come in—come in. Anything I can do for you, Mr. Cochran?

NICK: *(entering)* Maybe a lot—Mr. Halloran.

HALLORAN: *(shaking hands)* What's your problem—need a check cashed?

NICK: My problem is I need a bank account.

He notices his photo lying on top of the desk. He picks it up, looks questioningly at Halloran.

NICK: *(continued)* Were you thinking of having me framed?

HALLORAN: I like to keep posted on every potential customer.

NICK: I want to do business on the other side of the table. Got a job for me?

HALLORAN: What kind of training have you had for a job around here?

NICK: You want it long or short?

HALLORAN: Take your time.

NICK: I worked in a gambling house in Singapore . . .

HALLORAN: Why'd you quit?

NICK: I broke a house rule—let a heavy better win.

HALLORAN: The same house rule applies here. After Singapore?

NICK: Played nursemaid to a load of machine guns to Iraq. Moved on to Cairo—got rid of a handful of stones for a couple refugees who wanted visas.

HALLORAN: Hot merchandise?

NICK: For a change—this was on the level. *(then)* Blew that dough on slow horses—so I worked my way back to China on a freighter—and here I am—broke, and ready to go on your payroll.

HALLORAN: Doing what? I've got too many croupiers and dicemen already.

NICK: Maybe you need a skipper on your trips to Hong Kong? I can sail anything on water.

HALLORAN: *(blandly)* You must have heard that I never go beyond the three-mile limit. Didn't they tell you in New York?

NICK: I haven't seen New York in five years.

HALLORAN: Really—*(after a pause)*—Lieutenant?

NICK: Why the Lieutenant?

HALLORAN: My friend Lieutenant Sebastian of the police told me of your commission—in the Army. *(looking at him steadily)* Now there's a job you might have talent for—on the police force.

NICK: I'm not partial to the law. That's why I left the States—got into a jam.

HALLORAN: How long ago was that?

NICK: *(beginning to get impatient)* I told you—five years ago—in New York.

HALLORAN: *(with mock apology)* It's hard to remember all the details—of your career. What kind of a jam—you knock somebody off?

NICK: No—*you'd* call it small-time stuff.

HALLORAN: *(sardonically)* Smuggling arms ... getting rid of hot jewelry—that's too big-time for me. Sorry I can't do anything around here for you, Lieutenant.

NICK: Thanks anyway—I'll try one of the spots down the street.

HALLORAN: I doubt if there's a job in this town. You'd be smart to grab the next boat back to Hong Kong.

NICK: What do I use for money?

HALLORAN: *(holding out his hand—lightly)* I'll give it some thought.
Nick moves to the door. He comes face-to-face with Itzumi, who is holding the door open for him.

NICK: *(to Itzumi)* You talk too much.
Nick goes out. Halloran's face is no longer friendly.

UPPER GALLERY
As Nick moves toward the staircase. He passes Gimpy's room. Classical music floats out from behind the closed door. Camera holds on Gimpy's door.

INTERIOR GIMPY'S ROOM
It is a grimy room, made cheerful by Gimpy's collection of Oriental ancient instruments, hanging on the wall. An old upright piano stands in the corner. Gimpy is playing with exquisite interpretation. Julie, who has been looking at the collection of old instruments, turns and comes to the piano.

JULIE: *(as she watches him play)* Why does a long-hair like you play piano in a place like this?

32

Gimpy smiles and goes on playing.
JULIE: *(continued) (embarrassed, laughs)* I guess I shouldn't have asked. It's better than selling fish or begging.
GIMPY: *(wryly)* Only at times—like this. *(with a jazz flourish on the piano)* Shall we go through our extensive library?
He chooses a sheet of music and begins to play slowly.

INTERIOR QUICK REWARD—LOWER FLOOR
Nick has been standing, watching a table of fan-tan. Suddenly Julie's voice is heard, singing a melody with confidence. He cocks his head—all attention. He likes what he hears. Margie is running the table, acting as croupier. She takes Nick in.
MARGIE: I don't believe I've seen you before.
NICK: How do I look?
MARGIE: Basically, like every other man. *(indicating table)* Do you gamble?
NICK: Do you?
MARGIE: On anything.
NICK: Ever win?
MARGIE: *(with a smile)* No—I always lose.
NICK: You and me both.
Still looking at her, Nick takes a coin and places it on a square. The wrong number comes up.
MARGIE: Try again?
NICK: If I get in the mood, who do I ask for?
MARGIE: Margie . . .
NICK: No phone number?
MARGIE: There's a sign on me reading "Don't handle the merchandise."
NICK: I was just window-shopping.
Nick moves slowly toward the door, still listening to Julie's voice.

EXTERIOR THE QUICK REWARD
A large, powerful White Russian doorman is trying to drive away a group of beggars, who have collected outside.
DOORMAN: *(lifting his arms threateningly—in Portuguese)* Out of here before I call the police!

33

The beggars continue to shout at him.

DOORMAN: *(continued) (in assorted languages)* Get on your chopsticks, and beat it! Go on—away! I'll have you all jailed! *(etc.)*

They all scatter except one—Kwan Sum Tang, the blind man— who stumbles over his stick and drops it. Nick comes out. The doorman is in the act of breaking the blind man's cane in two.

NICK: *(quietly to doorman)* Take it easy. You could strain yourself doing that.

Nick takes the cane from him, hands the stick to the helpless beggar.

NICK: *(continued) (dropping a coin in his cup)* Are you all right?

The beggar smiles. Nick puts two fingers in his mouth, whistles for a ricksha.

NICK: *(continued) (to doorman)* What'd you do with all the rickshas, frighten them away, too?

He moves on down the street.

DOLLY SHOT—NICK

As he walks along. Suddenly a shot is heard very close to him, then another. Instinctively, he crouches.

TWO CHINESE KIDS

They are crouched in a doorway. One of them is holding a chain of sputtering firecrackers. The other has a stick of punk ready to light more firecrackers.

NICK

He grins and continues on. At a sound, he looks up, ducks away, just misses being hit by a huge pot of flowers which smashes on the sidewalk. He comes to the curb, is about to take a step when the screech of a car coming around the corner fills the screen. The car misses Nick by inches. He jumps out of the way. The roar of the car blots out the sound of Nick's voice, as he curses the car in no uncertain terms.

REAR OF CAR

As it speeds away.

BACK WINDOW OF CAR
Sebastian's face can be seen looking back at Nick. He smiles coolly, and salutes Nick.

NICK
He looks at his suit, splattered with mud from the wheels of the car. He backs away, bumps into a solid body. It is Trumble.
TRUMBLE: That was close!
Good-naturedly he tries to brush the mud off Nick's coat.
NICK: What a cleaning bill you can run up in this town! I haven't got enough problems.
TRUMBLE: Tell Mr. Anthony all about 'em over lunch.
Nick nods as they start walking . . .

DISSOLVE

INTERIOR QUICK REWARD—NIGHT
Gambling is at a frenzy. Sounds of the cries of the croupiers, dice, fan-tan buttons, and murmuring of the packed house. The lower floor is jammed. At tables along the upper gallery sit the well-dressed men and women of all nations, being served food and drink as they gamble through the pits. Gimpy's orchestra is playing. Halloran stands looking over the balcony, taking in the house. Margie is by his side.

GIMPY PLAYING PIANO
As he cues the orchestra to start Julie's first number, "You Kill Me." Camera pans to reveal Julie. She looks breathtaking in a low-cut grown. The spotlight illuminates her. She begins to sing.

HALLORAN AND MARGIE
As Halloran stares at Julie, obviously interested. Margie watches Halloran's face.

FAN-TAN PLAYERS
They stop playing at the tables, look up, listen. But only for a second. Nothing ever stops a gambler for long.

EURASIAN GIRLS AND CHINESE GAMBLERS
Betting, scarcely watching singer.

DUTCH TOURIST
He is fat. He stares at the singer with desire in his languorous eyes.

JULIE
Singing in professional nightclub style. She smiles at Halloran, and since he is the only one in the place whom she knows, she sings the lyrics to him.

ITZUMI
He is standing with several of Halloran's thugs, close to Halloran's office. His face has no expression.

MARGIE
Her eyes narrow imperceptibly.

HALLORAN
He is quite surprised at the style and charm that Julie has in putting a song across. Beyond this his eyes never leave the tight-fitting dress.

TRUMBLE
He is at the dice table below. He looks up, smiles, is pleased to hear and see Julie.

NICK FROM JULIE'S EYELINE
He is coming up the stairs.

HALLORAN
His face freezes as he sees Nick.

STAIR LANDING

As Nick arrives on the stair landing, Sebastian is only a step behind him. Sebastian stands by Nick's side. For a second both men observe Julie and listen to her.

JULIE
As she continues singing to Halloran, oblivious of the fact that Nick has arrived.

HALLORAN
His proprietary interest in Julie is obvious.

NICK AND SEBASTIAN
The policeman watches Nick's reactions shrewdly.
SEBASTIAN: As you can see, Lieutenant, my friend Halloran has diversified interests.
Nick looks at him, then at Julie.

JULIE
As she finishes her number. She looks in the direction of someone applauding.

STAIR LANDING FROM JULIE'S EYELINE
It is Sebastian who has applauded. Nick is no longer standing beside him.

JULIE
JULIE: *(turning to Gimpy)* Are they always that enthusiastic?
GIMPY: *(still playing)* Always.

LOWER FLOOR—GAMBLING TABLE
Crowd of players are watching Margie. As the croupier, she scoops up Trumble's money, which the salesman has just lost in a dice throw.
MARGIE: *(raking)* The house wins—you lose. Try again?
TRUMBLE: *(waving a fistful of greenbacks)* Sure. The night's young— I've got lots of cabbage in my garden!

37

*Trumble is about to make another throw when Nick comes down
the stairs.*

TRUMBLE: *(continued) (offering him a bill)* Come on—try your luck,
Nick! This Chinese three-dice game is a pushover! You just bet on the
number of points that come up.

NICK: *(his eyes roaming the room)* No, thanks—

TRUMBLE: *(indicating upstairs)* She sings plenty easy.

NICK: Yes. Like she makes new friends.

TRUMBLE: Well, easy come, easy go. Like my bankroll. Sure you
don't want to try your luck?

NICK: Not the way it's running.

HALLORAN'S VOICE: Why not, Mr. Cochran?
Halloran walks into scene as they turn.

HALLORAN: *(continued)* I've got a feeling this is your night. You
know, the dice run hot when love grows cold.

NICK: What do you suggest—*(holding up bill)*—to turn my last ten
into a pot of gold?

HALLORAN: Roll three sixes and you get thirty-five to one.

NICK: How often does that happen?

HALLORAN: I've got a hunch it might happen right now.
*Nick shrugs, kisses the ten-dollar bill, and places it on the proper
dice combination. (Throughout the scene it is evident that Nick is
aware that Halloran is deliberately creating this tension.)*

NICK: Shoot the works.
Margie offers Nick the tray of dice.

NICK: *(continued) (shaking his head)* You know 'em better than I do.
*Margie takes out three dice, drops them into the dice cup, blows
softly on them, gives Halloran a knowing look, and rolls the dice
out.*

INSERT   DICE ON TABLE
As they come to a stop, disclosing all three are sixes.
Back to scene as the crowd around the table reacts.

TRUMBLE: Lady Luck didn't just smile on you—she got hysterical!

NICK: *(to Halloran)* Who do you get your hunches from?

HALLORAN: *(to stickman)* Pay the man. Three hundred and fifty
dollars.

38

The stickman counts out the money over Nick's ten.
HALLORAN: *(continued) (stopping Nick as he reaches for the dough)*
Let it ride, Lieutenant. On the triple-six.
NICK: *(after a long pause)* Let it ride.
The stickman rakes in the dice and shoves them toward Margie.
She scoops them up into her hand.
MARGIE: Same dice?
Nick looks at Halloran for the decision.
HALLORAN: Why change now?
NICK: *(to Margie)* Same dice.
Again she drops them in the dice cup, blows softly on the dice, rolls
them out.

INSERT   DICE ON TABLE
As they bounce off the edge, revealing three sixes when they stop.
Back to scene—Nick wipes the sweat from his brow, as the crowd
reacts and grows larger. Halloran exchanges a look with Margie.
TRUMBLE: I see it, but I don't believe it! Six sixes in a row! *(turning to*
Nick) Thirty-five times three fifty ... *(adding mentally—then)—*
that's—I'm afraid to figure it!
By this time the stickman has piled a stack of bills on the triple-
six.
STICKMAN: Twelve thousand, two hundred and fifty dollars.
NICK: Mr. Halloran—I never want to lose *you.*
HALLORAN: I'm sure you don't.
Nick reaches out to get his money.
HALLORAN: *(continued)* I thought you were a gambler.
NICK: *(stopping his gesture halfway)* Don't tell me to let it all ride!
HALLORAN: How often in a lifetime does a man have a streak like
this? Hit the point once more—and you're a rich man.
Nick hesitates, apparently tempted. He eyes Trumble.
TRUMBLE: Don't look at me.
Nick turns to Margie, who smiles at him enigmatically.
NICK: *(after a deep breath; to Halloran)* It's your money. Let it ride.
(reaching into pile of money) All except this. *(handing bill to Trumble)*
The twenty I owe you.
Trumble takes the bill as Nick turns back to Margie.

NICK: *(continued)* Roll 'em. The same dice. And, if you please, the same numbers—

The stickman shoves the dice to Margie, who drops them in the dice cup, blows on them, shakes the box slowly, then rolls dice out.

INSERT   DICE ON TABLE

Two of the dice stop, showing sixes. The third die is still spinning on its point, then finally comes to a stop, disclosing a one.
Back to scene as the crowd gasps. Nick brushes his hands together as if to wipe the dust off them.

NICK: *(continued) (to Margie)* Nice try.

TRUMBLE: *(offering bill to Nick)* You owe me twenty.

Nick takes it ruefully, turns to Halloran.

NICK: Any other ideas to liven up the evening?

HALLORAN: I might have.

NICK: *(starts off with him, then turns back to table and scoops up the three dice)* Mind if I keep these—souvenirs?

They start off as Trumble eyes them, then turns back to the table.

TRUMBLE: Fifty cents on the triple-six. What can I lose?

Nick and Halloran as they walk to a quiet part of the floor.

HALLORAN: *(casually)* Taking the advice I gave you this afternoon?

NICK: I haven't decided.

HALLORAN: Would you go if you hadn't made that last throw of the dice?

NICK: And keep the twelve thousand?

HALLORAN: Let's say half of it. A man like you could do a lot with that—back in New York. *(crisply)* Pick up the money and your ticket to Hong Kong in my office tomorrow morning—in time to take the noon ferry.

He leaves, as Nick looks after him thoughtfully. Then be begins to walk toward the door.

JULIE'S VOICE: Hi!

NICK: *(turning)* Hi!

Julie comes into scene, dressed for the street.

JULIE: Like my song?

NICK: *(without warmth)* The song was fine.

JULIE: What's the matter?

40

NICK: Not a thing. I'm planning to pull out of here tomorrow.
JULIE: When will you be back?
NICK: Don't keep a light burning in the window.
Nick walks out.

EXTERIOR QUICK REWARD
Nick comes out. The doorman disregards him. Nick signals for a ricksha, whistles impatiently. He pulls out a cigarette, searches through his pockets for a match. Julie appears behind him.
JULIE: Looking for me?
Ricksha pulls into scene and Nick moves toward it.
JULIE: *(continued)* Do you mind giving me a lift to the hotel?
NICK: *(hesitating momentarily)* Climb in.
Julie gets into the ricksha, followed by Nick. The ricksha goes off.

UPPER-FLOOR WINDOW
Halloran is standing at the window looking down, reacts to Julie and Nick going off together.

DISSOLVE

NICK AND JULIE IN RICKSHA—NIGHT (PROCESS)
Nick's continued coolness perplexes Julie.
JULIE: Isn't your leaving Macao kind of sudden?
NICK: A good proposition came up. I can't afford to turn it down.
JULIE: Then this hasn't been such a bad place for you.
NICK: Hasn't been tough for you either. You broke the bank, as far as Halloran is concerned.
JULIE: *(defensively)* He pays my salary, that's all.
NICK: Sure—but does *he* figure it that way?
JULIE: Look—*I* pick my men—I don't let them pick me.
NICK: It's a good theory—does it work?
JULIE: *(ruefully)* No . . . *(hopefully)* But it might some day—
NICK: Who have you got in mind this time?
JULIE: Well, I'll tell you one thing, it isn't Halloran—*(as Nick grins)*—and it isn't you.

41

NICK: I can keep a secret. Who is it—that stocking salesman who wooed you with his fancy nylons?
JULIE: Nylons come in handy.
NICK: I know. I used a pair of 'em once to get out of a second-story window.
JULIE: Was she pretty?
NICK: I never noticed. It was dark. *(looking at watch)* It's too early to turn in. Why don't you grab a coat at the hotel and we go for a sampan ride? I talk very convincingly in a sampan.
JULIE: Do you have any other ideas?
NICK: None that you couldn't handle.

DISSOLVE

EXTERIOR DOCK—NIGHT
Beyond we can see the sampans, the dock, and the moon on the harbor. Itzumi stands looking out over the water.

DISSOLVE

THE HARBOR—NIGHT
Showing colorful array of boats and sails. Faintly we hear the opening strains of "Ocean Breeze."

THE SAMPAN
As it moves along the water to the slap-slap of the oar. The oarsman behind them pushes the long oar into the water rhythmically. Julie's voice is heard singing "Ocean Breeze."

NICK AND JULIE
They lie side by side in the sampan. Julie's phonograph near them is playing Julie's record.

MOVING SHOT—LINE OF SAMPANS
As our sampan glides through the harbor corridors of the sampan village, we see:

42

a. *Chinese family. On this first sampan a young Chinese mother with her infant in her arms singing a Chinese lullaby to it.*
b. *Second Chinese family. They are asleep on deck—several children, the mother, the father.*
c. *Young Chinese couple. They are embracing.*

JULIE AND NICK
As the vocal part of the record finishes and goes into orchestral accompaniment.

JULIE: I'd swap twenty Chinese moons for one over the East River . . .

NICK: Or the Hudson. You know the little twenty-four-dollar island well?

JULIE: I was born there—went to school there. I can even remember the dump I lived in when I was a kid. *(cynically)* One day my old lady bought some wax fruit and put it in a cut-glass bowl on what passed for our dining room table. I got hungry and bit into one of the apples. *(with a bitter laugh)* That's me all over—always biting phony apples . . .

NICK: *(quietly)* What brought you out here?

JULIE: My talent—my talent for picking the wrong guy . . .

NICK: That's a break for me—or tonight you'd be cooking dinner for some other mug while the kids are down with the measles—the icebox doesn't work—there's a knock on the door and the landlord says the rent's overdue—the neighbors are having a little discussion downstairs that comes over the dumbwaiter blow-by-blow—and that mug you married had a hard day at the office and he wants you to help him forget all about it.

JULIE: Is that bad?

NICK: I don't like office work.

JULIE: *(trying to be casual)* Where are you headed for tomorrow?

NICK: *(shrugging)* East—north—south—west—all the points of the compass. Take your choice.

JULIE: Funny—this is good-bye and all I know about you is—your name—and that you can swim . . .

43

NICK: I'll tell you more about me. I like to be on the go. I don't like to be handcuffed to anything—or anybody!

There is a pause.

JULIE: *(slowly)* When are you leaving?

NICK: The noon ferry.

They look at each other.

NICK: *(continued) (quietly)* I don't suppose—you'd come along with me.

JULIE: No, thanks. I'm like you. Have all the fun—and no responsibilities.

NICK: Sure.

A pause.

NICK: *(continued)* Would you have any strenuous objections to a good-bye kiss?

JULIE: None that you couldn't handle.

He takes her in his arms. There is a long kiss.

LONG SHOT—HARBOR
The sampan in which Julie and Nick are locked in each other's arms has now blended into the hundreds of floating villages, bobbing on the moonlit waters of Macao . . .

FADE OUT

FADE IN

LONG SHOT—DOCKS AND HARBOR—MORNING
Another sunny day in Macao . . . activity on the water. Cathedral chimes.

INTERIOR HOTEL PORTUGUEZA CORRIDOR
As Trumble comes down from his floor and walks up to Nick's door. He is about to knock when he notices something in front of the door.

CLOSE SHOT—SMALL VASE OF FLOWERS

44

A note is attached. Camera moves up as Trumble's hand lifts up the vase and takes the folded note from the flowers. He has a battle with his conscience whether to read the note or not. He opens the note.

INSERT   NOTE
In Julie's handwriting: "JULIE"

Back to scene—Trumble, grinning, knocks on Nick's door.
NICK'S VOICE: *(offstage)* Come in.
Trumble enters with the vase.

INTERIOR NICK'S ROOM
Nick has almost finished shaving. Trumble enters.
NICK: Greetings. Who sent you the posies?
TRUMBLE: Me? The only time I'll ever get flowers will be at my funeral. They're for you.
Nick takes the carnations and reads the note.
NICK: Bet you the twenty I owe you that you'll never guess who sent these.
TRUMBLE: It's a bet if I had the twenty. I should have left with you last night.
NICK: You went to the cleaners?
TRUMBLE: And how. Too bad you didn't hit that last triple-six.
NICK: *(putting on his shirt)* I can still collect half of the dough I won on my second roll. *(as Trumble looks at him questioningly)* All I have to do is pick up the six thousand from Halloran—and take the noon boat.
TRUMBLE: All I have to do is believe you.
NICK: I'm serious.
TRUMBLE: *(astounded)* Are you trying to say that Halloran will give you all that moola just to get out of town?
NICK: That's right.
TRUMBLE: For that kind of money I'd swim back to Hong Kong. What's his idea?

45

NICK: He wants a clear field with Julie, is my guess. Figures he'll make a big man of himself with her by running me out of town in first-class style.

TRUMBLE: What time you leaving?

NICK: *(looking at flowers)* I'm not.

TRUMBLE: *(shrewdly)* As long as you've decided to stay here, I think you and I can do some business together.

He pulls a large glittering pear-shaped diamond out of his pocket.

TRUMBLE: *(continued)* Our capital. This belongs to a necklace of fourteen-carat stones. Twenty of 'em—all perfect whites.

NICK: *(whistles)* Where'd you get it?

TRUMBLE: Sideline of mine. The necklace is in Hong Kong—in a safe deposit box at the Grand Hotel—

NICK: It sizzles like a fried egg.

TRUMBLE: Don't worry—it's cool enough to be sold. Original price—a hundred thousand. I'll take forty—and if you sell 'em, I'll give you ten percent.

NICK: *(figuring)* Ten percent? That's four thousand.

TRUMBLE: Four thousand.

NICK: *(tying his tie, shrewdly)* Why do you want *me* to play middleman for you?

TRUMBLE: Can't do it myself. I don't want to mix it up with my legitimate business.

NICK: *(sardonically)* What old dowager is going to hand me forty thousand for this—and no questions asked?

TRUMBLE: I figure Halloran fits the part.

NICK: *(after reflection)* Why not—I've got a date with him this morning anyhow.

Nick puts on his coat, sticks one of Julie's carnations in his buttonhole.

TRUMBLE: Tell him where the rest of the necklace is. If he wants to make a deal, it's got to be cash—in your hands—in Hong Kong.

NICK: *(tossing stone in his hand)* How do you know I won't run out on you?

TRUMBLE: I don't . . .

DISSOLVE

INTERIOR LOWER FLOOR QUICK REWARD—
MORNING
*As Nick enters. It is early morning, and the place is still inactive. A
couple of Chinese are cleaning up. Only one table is going, with a
Chinese placing bets against the house. Sound of classical music
is heard from upstairs as Nick walks up.*

UPPER GALLERY QUICK REWARD
*As Nick approaches Gimpy's open door, we can see Gimpy at the
piano. Margie is leaning against the piano with a faraway look.*

INTERIOR GIMPY'S ROOM
As Nick enters. Gimpy continues to play.
NICK: Ah—the lady of the loaded dice. *(as she turns)* Good morning.
MARGIE: You're up early for a loser.
NICK: Can't make a dishonest dollar lying in bed. Halloran around?
MARGIE: He's busy counting out your dowry. All set to go?
NICK: Got a better offer?
MARGIE: I'm a one-man-at-a-time woman.
NICK: You go right on believing it—like they all do. Could you tear
yourself away long enough to tell Mr. Triple-Six I'm here and to bring
his money belt with him?
MARGIE: What's your hurry?
Nick takes a folded handkerchief out of his pocket.
NICK: This is burning a hole in my pocket.
*He takes the pendant out of the handkerchief and holds it up.
Margie reacts, her hand goes toward the stone. Casually Nick
hands it to her.*
NICK: Part of the family fortune.
*She turns to go, but Nick catches her by the wrist and takes the
pendant.*
NICK: *(continued)* My calling card.
*Margie exits swiftly. Nick comes to the piano and leans against it.
He takes out a cigarette. As Gimpy continues playing, Nick
borrows Gimpy's lighted cigarette to light his own, then puts it
back into the piano player's mouth. At this moment Margie*

47

enters, followed by Halloran and Itzumi. Gimpy immediately stops playing.

HALLORAN: *(dryly)* I hear you've come into money. And I was worried you didn't have enough to buy yourself a ferryboat ride . . .

NICK: *(lightly)* Oh—you mean this little trinket? It's nothing.

Nick draws the pendant diamond from his pocket, holds it up to the light between his thumb and forefinger.

NICK: *(continued) (with deliberate formality)* This usually hangs on for dear life to a necklace of twenty flawless, fourteen-carat diamonds.

Halloran recognizes the pendant, reacts. Nick flips the diamond to him as though it were a marble. Halloran catches it.

HALLORAN: *(too casually)* Where did you pick it up?

NICK: *(smiling)* Out of a high silk hat. I use diamonds instead of rabbits.

HALLORAN: How much?

NICK: *(matter-of-fact)* The pendant and the necklace are appraised at a hundred grand.

HALLORAN: I wouldn't be a bit surprised.

NICK: But I'll let them find a new home for forty thousand.

HALLORAN: I'm always in the market for first-rate stuff . . . *(to Margie)* Like it?

MARGIE: What good would it do me if I did?

HALLORAN: *(to Nick)* Where's the necklace?

NICK: I left it in Hong Kong. Careless of me, wasn't it?

A look is exchanged between Itzumi and Halloran. Casually Nick holds out his hand. Halloran hands back the stone.

HALLORAN: *(to Nick)* We might make a deal. Why don't you pick up the necklance and bring it back here?

NICK: The deal has to be closed in Hong Kong. You've got too many close friends in Macao.

HALLORAN: Itzumi, you feel like a trip?

ITZUMI: The boat is ready.

NICK: *(blandly, to Halloran)* Do you think it's a good idea—going on a blind date with a hatchet-man? I don't. *You*'ll have to go to Hong Kong with me.

Gimpy resumes playing as Nick holds up the pendant. Camera moves close on the stone until it fills the screen with its glittering surface.

DISSOLVE

INTERIOR TRUMBLE'S HOTEL ROOM—DAY
Trumble is fiddling around with some fishing equipment. A knock sounds at the door.
TRUMBLE: Come in.
Nick enters.
TRUMBLE: *(continued)* How'd you make out?
NICK: We're in business.
TRUMBLE: Price okay?
NICK: No argument. I'm meeting Halloran at the dock at 9:30 tonight. We're taking his boat.
TRUMBLE: Better be careful. His crew might jump you.
NICK: There won't be a crew. The two of us are going alone.
TRUMBLE: Nice work.
He goes to the desk, brings out a revolver and hands it to Nick.
NICK: I was just going to ask you where I could borrow one.
TRUMBLE: Another sideline.
Nick cracks open the gun, examines it while Trumble is reaching into drawer under some shirts for something. Nick has the gun pointed very close to Trumble's temple, as Trumble turns.
TRUMBLE: *(continued) (reacts, pushes gun away)* Here's the key to the safe deposit box at the Grand Hotel. Ask for Mr. Stewart—I'll cable him you're coming. *(hands him key)*
NICK: I ought to be back in the morning.
Nick starts to exit.
TRUMBLE: By the way—Nick—*(as he turns at door)* Ever think of going home?
NICK: *(after a pause)* I can't go home any more than you can.
TRUMBLE: Why not?
NICK: *(tersely, after a moment's hesitation)* A little hassle over a redhead. Somebody fired a shot. It turned out to be me.

49

TRUMBLE: The other guy die?

NICK: No—but I got to China before I found *that* out. Then I just kept going—looking for a perfect country.

TRUMBLE: You can't keep looking forever.

NICK: I sure can try.

TRUMBLE: A smart guy would go back and face the music.

NICK: I don't see you trying to clean up your own record.

TRUMBLE: I will—one of these days—or my name isn't Lawrence C. Trumble.

NICK: What does the "C" stand for?

TRUMBLE: Cicero—but keep it under your hat.

He goes out as Trumble looks after him thoughtfully, then turns back to his fishing rods.

INTERIOR HOTEL—SECOND-FLOOR LANDING

As Nick comes down from the third floor and runs into Julie on her way out.

NICK: *(ceremoniously)* I beg your pardon—but didn't you and I waltz together in a sampan last night?

JULIE: *(with pretense at elegance)* I hardly think we frequent the same social circles.

NICK: I could have sworn you were the conniving woman who sent me flowers this morning.

JULIE: Me? Send flowers to you? My dear man, you must be mad.

NICK: *(a la Barrymore)* Mad, she says! I will show this wench how mad I am!

He grabs Julie and is about to kiss her when a Chinese chambermaid comes into view with an armful of linen.

NICK: *(continued) (to chambermaid)* It's all right—we're not married.

Julie laughs and moves down the stairs as Nick follows after her.

THE LOBBY

As they come down stars. Nick waits while Julie deposits her key with the clerk.

NICK: Hey, what's the hurry? I was just about to indulge in a kiss.

JULIE: Before breakfast?

50

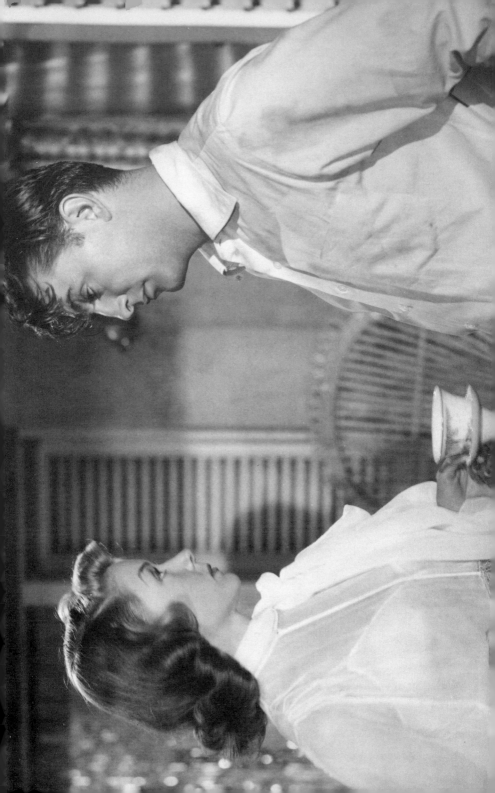

NICK: For breakfast!

JULIE: How utterly absurd! And keep a man waiting?

NICK: Don't trifle with me, damsel! Who is this varlet—I'll run him through!

JULIE: You do and you'll kill the best piano player in town—I've got to rehearse.

EXTERIOR HOTEL

As they come out, Nick whistles for a ricksha. Kwan Sum Tang stands outside the gate, and Julie drops a coin in his cup as they pass.

NICK: And here I was going to ply you with soft words and violent action.

JULIE: Won't they keep until tonight?

NICK: They'd have to keep until tomorrow. Tonight I'm going to Hong Kong—on a little deal.

JULIE: Blonde or brunette?

By now she has climbed into a ricksha, but Nick's hand on the seat detains the boy from drawing away.

NICK: You just gave me an idea—but unfortunately this trip is strictly business. *(looking steadily at her)* Do you really have to rehearse?

JULIE: Make me a better offer.

NICK: *(eyes on her)* Well—there must be a little spot up in the hills—there always is. We could pretend it's a dark night.

JULIE: Stop looking at me like that!

NICK: You're asking the impossible.

JULIE: *(laughing)* Whatever you're trying to do to me, do it some other time—(to driver) The Quick Reward—the quicker the better! *(to Nick)* See you tomorrow.

The ricksha moves away as we hold on Nick and the blind beggar, smiling.

DISSOLVE

EXTERIOR PUT-PUT—DAY (PROCESS)

Trumble in back of boat loaded with fishing equipment, leaving Macao harbor. He is accompanied by a coolie at the motor. He offers coolie a cigar and it is accepted with a thankful grin.

DISSOLVE

EXTERIOR BUOY AT SEA—DAY
The legend on it proclaims in Chinese and in English that it is the three-mile limit.

EXTERIOR OPEN WATERS—DAY
Power-boat approaches. On deck is a Britisher in tropical uniform, binoculars and basket-weave megaphone at hand.

EXTERIOR OPEN WATERS
Trumble is fishing.

EXTERIOR OPEN WATERS
The power boat approaches. The captain of the craft, Stewart, a lean, fine-looking Britisher in his forties, hails Trumble.
STEWART: Ahoy there! Are they biting today?
TRUMBLE: I heard there were sharks out here, but I'm ready to settle for a sardine.
STEWART: Careful of the sun. How about coming on board for a drink and some shade?
TRUMBLE: You don't have to ask me twice. *(handing the pole to his coolie)* Me catchee drinkee.
The coolie grins as the boats make contact and Trumble is hoisted aboard. By Stewart's side are two uniformed men, a Portuguese and a Chinese.

DECK OF POWERBOAT
As Stewart shakes hands with Trumble.
STEWART: *(shaking hands)* My name's Stewart. This is Senhor Alvaris—and Mr. Chang.
Trumble smiles in greeting and follows Stewart as he goes below.

52

INTERIOR CABIN—POWERBOAT

As they come in. The moment Stewart closes the door, he faces Trumble with a revolver.

STEWART: All right—your business?

TRUMBLE: Fishing.

STEWART: For what?

TRUMBLE: Shark.

STEWART: What kind?

TRUMBLE: Man-eater.

Stewart's face relaxes into a smile as he puts his gun away and extends his hand.

STEWART: Good to see you, Lieutenant Ryan. We've been on the look-see for you all day.

TRUMBLE: It's good to find you here, Captain Stewart.

STEWART: You fellows from New York don't care how far you sling your nets to catch one fish!

TRUMBLE: This one's a whopper.

Stewart moves to put out bottled water and Scotch as they talk.

STEWART: He must be. I wasn't here last year when your department sent that other chap out.

TRUMBLE: He made the mistake of letting Halloran know who he was. *(grimly)* Two days after he landed, he was found in the harbor—accidental drowning.

STEWART: I remember. Pal of yours?

TRUMBLE: Just another New York cop.

Stewart indicates to Trumble to help himself.

STEWART: *(as Trumble pours himself a glass of water)* Any luck so far?

TRUMBLE: He'll be in your hands by ten o'clock tonight.

STEWART: *(surprised)* How did you ever swing it? I didn't think anyone could get Halloran past the three-mile limit.

TRUMBLE: It took his own jewelry to do it. Last week he sent a messenger to Hong Kong with a diamond necklace. With the help of the British police, we grabbed the messenger, the necklace and the fence.

STEWART: Made him bait his own trap, eh?

53

TRUMBLE: Exactly. I took one of the stones with me. I was pretty sure Halloran would jump when he laid eyes on it, thinking he'd been double-crossed.

STEWART: And he's actually going to Hong Kong with you?

TRUMBLE: Not with me. With a friend of mine—Nick Cochran.

STEWART: Isn't it dangerous to let another man know about our job?

TRUMBLE: Cochran doesn't know a thing—except that he's selling a hundred-thousand-dollar necklace. I promised him four thousand that he'll never see.

STEWART: I hardly think he'll like it when he discovers he's been made a—?

TRUMBLE: A patsy? Frankly, I hated to fool him. But we can do our friend a good turn. Seems he got sidetracked back home in the States.

STEWART: Serious trouble?

TRUMBLE: Kid stuff. I have a feeling he'd give his right arm to go home and start from scratch.

STEWART: If he delivers Halloran to us, he'll be entitled to a clean slate. What time will I have the pleasure of receiving our distinguished guest?

TRUMBLE: You'll be sending Nick back to me with a receipt for Halloran by ten tonight.

The two men smile thoughtfully, toast glasses as we . . .

DISSOLVE

SECTION OF WATERFRONT—NIGHT
Close shot—sign, indicating Largo do Pagode da Barra. Camera draws back to reveal that the street sign is on the corner of an old building. The fog rolls in. Nick checks the sign by the light of a lamp post. He is wearing one of Julie's flowers. He pats the revolver in his back pocket, walks to the edge of the docks.

CLOSE SHOT—NICK
He takes out a package of cigarettes and is hunting for a match when the click of a cigarette lighter startles the quiet and a hand comes into scene, lighting Nick's cigarette by the flame of a gold lighter. Camera pulls back to reveal Halloran.

54

HALLORAN: I didn't keep you waiting?

NICK: I just got here myself.

Camera moves with Halloran and Nick as they begin to walk along the line of boats. Nick keeps looking around suspiciously.

HALLORAN: If you're looking for your girl friend, she won't be with you tonight.

NICK: *(reacting)* Oh—you know about last night? *(as Halloran nods)* That's the trouble with women—they always talk.

(thinking he's needling him) Tell me—how do you think I'm doing with her?

HALLORAN: We've got hours to discuss that. *(indicating)* Here's my boat.

NICK: Looks like she's got power. 220 h.p.?

HALLORAN: Add forty. She'll go fifty-five an hour. Can you take her out in this fog?

NICK: Why not—looks like it's clearing up—

At this moment a blackjack crashes down on his skull.

CLOSE SHOT—HALLORAN

As he stands watching, we hear Nick's body thud to the ground.

CLOSE SHOT—NICK

He is trying desperately not to lose consciousness, but his eyes are glazing. His hand reaches for his gun. A foot comes into scene, pressing down on his wrist. He looks up at Halloran.

HALLORAN

He is out of focus . . . blurred, distorted.

HALLORAN: What do you take me for—a small-time gunsel!

Halloran moves forward and picks Nick up by the lapels.

HALLORAN: *(continued)* I gave you an out—and a bundle of dough to go with it, but you wouldn't play!—Did you think I'd fall for a cheap police trick? I sent that necklace to Hong Kong a week ago.

Full shot revealing two henchmen—Orientals—large, powerful men, with Itzumi standing quietly in the background.

HALLORAN: Did you think I wouldn't recognize my own stuff when you brought it to me! Did you think I'd get in a boat and risk the three-

mile limit! *(loosens his grip, Nick slumps to ground)* You're not on Seventh Avenue! You're in Macao—this is my precinct!
As the henchmen move forward to pick up Nick . . .

DISSOLVE

EXTERIOR POLICE BOAT AT SEA—NIGHT
On board, Stewart is watching the ocean in vain through his binoculars. He looks at the boat clock. Camera pans to the clock. It says 10:30.

DISSOLVE

SECTION WATERFRONT—NIGHT
In the grayness can be heard the sound of running footsteps. Then Trumble hurries into scene. He looks around, hunting for Nick. Discovering no one here, he hurries away.

ANOTHER SECTION WATERFRONT
Again Trumble hurries into scene looking at the various boats. Then suddenly he sees something offstage and reacts.

HALLORAN'S BOAT MOORED AT THE DOCK

TRUMBLE
As he hurries to Halloran's boat he looks around to be sure that no one is watching him, then boards boat.

INTERIOR HALLORAN'S BOAT
Trumble gets busy. He rummages until he finds a flashlight, plays it on the woodwork.

INSERT   OWNERSHIP REGISTRATION
It is a Macao license affirming that Vincent Halloran is the owner of the boat.

TRUMBLE

He turns his attention to the motor, feel it, realizes it is cold. He listens to see if all is safe. Then, seeing a small cabinet, he tries the knob. It is locked. He finds a wrench, wrenches the door open. He discovers a wireless communication set, which he proceeds to use.

INTERIOR POLICE BOAT
As Stewart listens carefully to the wireless. An operator is at the set.

INTERIOR HALLORAN'S BOAT
Trumble is tapping out his message in Morse code when he suddenly hears the rhythmic, ominous tapping of a cane. He signals for a pause and exits from the cabin, closing the door to set hurriedly.

EXTERIOR HALLORAN'S BOAT
As Trumble, on the alert, emerges. The tapping comes closer and he sees:

EXTERIOR WATERFRONT
Kwan Sum Tang, the blind beggar, comes out of the fog. Trumble climbs from the boat and walks close to him. The beggar stops, as if sensing interference.

KWAN: *(in Chinese)* Who is there?
TRUMBLE: *(dropping coin in cup)* Just a tourist. You live near here?
KWAN: I live in a sampan—like most of us.
TRUMBLE: Did you hear a boat leave in the last hour or so—a motorboat?
KWAN: No. They never went aboard.
TRUMBLE: Who's "they?"
KWAN: There was a fight. The young American and the master of the Quick Reward.
TRUMBLE: Was anyone hurt?
The beggar turns and Trumble follows him. They arrive at the spot where Nick fell to the ground. Trumble looks around. His eyes fix on the ground.

CLOSE SHOT—CARNATION
As Trumble bends to find the flower he noticed in Nick's buttonhole that morning. Camera draws back as Trumble draws his finger across a trace of blood that he finds on the ground.

DISSOLVE

INTERIOR UPPER GALLERY QUICK REWARD—NIGHT
Itzumi is opening the door to Halloran's office for Julie. She is dressed to sing her next number.

INTERIOR HALLORAN'S OFFICE
As Julie comes in. He is looking out the window, turns as she enters.
JULIE: Yes, Mr. Halloran? I was about to go on.
HALLORAN: No hurry.
JULIE: You're the boss.
HALLORAN: So was Genghis Khan. Ever hear of him?
JULIE: Competitor of yours?
HALLORAN: He was the number one man around here a long time ago.
JULIE: And now *you* are.
HALLORAN: I used to steal fruit from the peddlers on Grand Avenue because I couldn't afford a decent meal—tonight I'm Emperor of Macao!
JULIE: Just what are you celebrating tonight?
HALLORAN: My freedom. How about celebrating together?
JULIE: How?
HALLORAN: *(pointing out window)* We can start with a ride on my boat.
JULIE: Some other time.
HALLORAN: Maybe you prefer a sampan.
JULIE: Maybe—Mr. Halloran.
HALLORAN: How long did it take you to call him Nick last night?
JULIE: To me a sampan is just a taxi on water, that's all.
HALLORAN: That's all?

58

JULIE: He wanted to say good-bye. He was going away. He was broke—couldn't get a job . . .

HALLORAN: And I thought you were a smart girl.

JULIE: No girl is smart enough not to fall in love.

HALLORAN: I thought you were.

JULIE: Well, I wasn't.

HALLORAN: What if he walked out on you?

JULIE: Only as far as Hong Kong—he'll be back in the morning.

HALLORAN: What if I told you he never went to Hong Kong?

JULIE: I'm sure he did.

HALLORAN: Look, Julie, I like you—more than I want to. So let me set you straight on Mr. Nick Cochran—*(with sarcasm)*—who was broke and couldn't get a job. He's a detective—New York Police Department—sent out here with orders to bring me back—dead or alive. He was just building himself up with you so you'd help him take me in.

JULIE: I don't believe he's a cop.

HALLORAN: What makes you think I'm a liar?

JULIE: I want to hear what Nick says when he gets back tomorrow morning.

HALLORAN: When he doesn't show—and you're convinced he's been playing a double game, have we got a date for a boat ride?

JULIE: *(after a pause)* Maybe . . .

She turns and goes out.

UPPER GALLERY QUICK REWARD

Julie comes out, obviously troubled. She turns as Trumble approaches.

TRUMBLE: *(hiding his concern)* Hello, Miss Benton. Seen Nick?

JULIE: He told *me* he was going to Hong Kong. Did he say anything to you?

TRUMBLE: I wouldn't know. Maybe he's got another girl!

JULIE: From what I just heard, anything's possible.

TRUMBLE: What'd you hear?

JULIE: *(troubled)* Halloran just told me Nick's a New York cop.

TRUMBLE: *(putting it on big)* A cop? He's not dumb enough for that.

59

JULIE: But I'm just dumb enough to fall for the line he handed me last night. Excuse me—my public waits.

She hurries off. Trumble looks after her thoughtfully, then goes to Halloran's open office door.

INTERIOR HALLORAN'S OFFICE
As Trumble enters.

HALLORAN: Hello, Mr. Trumble. Sorry you had bad luck last night. Anything I can do for you?

TRUMBLE: Yeah—tell me how I can be such a dope about people.

HALLORAN: Who do you mean?

TRUMBLE: Your girl friend just told me about Cochran. Did he take me in!

HALLORAN: Did he now!

TRUMBLE: Where do you suppose the guy is now?

HALLORAN: Why are you so interested?

TRUMBLE: *(ruefully)* I loaned him twenty bucks.

HALLORAN: I hope *we've* beat you for more than that.

TRUMBLE: You can take me for more—if you'll cash a check.

HALLORAN: Sure—the only way to win is to keep on playing. How much do you want?

TRUMBLE: About four hundred.

HALLORAN: References?

TRUMBLE: *(pulling out wallet)* All you want.

INTERIOR UPPER GALLERY—JULIE AND GIMPY
As she sits on the piano and sings "One for My Baby."

TRUMBLE AND HALLORAN
As they come out, stop to listen to her sing.

PATRONS
They are here tonight again—the wealthy Orientals—the dissipated tourists—the languorous Dutchman—and his girl.

JULIE

60

As she sings, the hurt expression in her face, the lyrics she sings, the way she sings the song—all point up the conflict that is going on within her.

DIRECTOR'S PICKUP SHOTS
They cover Julie's "torch" number—including audience reactions, especially Halloran's, until she finishes her song.

FADE OUT

FADE IN

MACAO—MORNING
Shots to establish that another day has begun.

CATHEDRAL TOWER
As the chimes carol ten o'clock.

RUA DA FELICIDADE
As Sebastian's car comes rushing over the cobblestones, scaring pedestrians, chickens, and dogs alike.

EXTERIOR QUICK REWARD
As Sebastian's car stops with a screech in front of the entrance. Pale and shaken, Sebastian hurries from the car and into the gambling house.

LOWER FLOOR QUICK REWARD
It is so early in the morning that there is only one man gambling. Servants are cleaning up the place. Sebastian rushes up the stairs.

INTERIOR HALLORAN'S OFFICE
Halloran sits at his desk, fingering the diamond. He looks at the pendant, then at the dock photograph of Julie, which has been placed in a silver frame on his desk. He strikes a match and lights his cigarette. Sebastian bursts in and tries to find his breath.
HALLORAN: Who's chasing *you?*

61

SEBASTIAN: Have you ever heard of the American marines?

He draws out a cablegram.

SEBASTIAN: *(continued) (reading)* "Commissioner of Police, Macao. You are advised Mr. Nick Cochran, an American, has been reported missing as of last night. He is under the protection of this Consulate and we would appreciate your cooperation regarding his whereabouts." *(as he finishes reading—with a deep sigh)* Signed by the American consul in Hong Kong.

HALLORAN: *(worried)* When did it arrive?

SEBASTIAN: Fifteen minutes ago.

HALLORAN: Get on the phone. Find out who cabled Hong Kong about Cochran.

Sebastian grabs the phone.

SEBASTIAN: *(at phone)* This is Lieutenant Felizardo José Espirito—

HALLORAN: *(snapping)* Take off the gold braid!

SEBASTIAN: *(meekly)* This is Lieutenant Sebastian. Get me the cable office.

He waits as Halloran moves restlessly.

SEBASTIAN: *(continued) (at phone)* This is Lieutenant Sebastian. I want a list of everyone who sent a cablegram in the last twenty-four hours. *(raising his voice)* A list! The entire list! *(shouting)* Don't tell me not to scream! I will scream as much as I please!—How many went out—who sent them! Every single name! *(as he listens, reacts)* Oh! *(sighs, hangs up)* No cables went out in the last twenty-four hours.

HALLORAN: We don't raise carrier pigeons on this island! Find out what boats left the harbor during the night!

Sebastian nods and hurries out.

DISSOLVE

WATERFRONT RESIDENTIAL DISTRICT—MORNING

As Kwan Sum Tang taps his way along the cobblestones. He passes Margie's house. Suddenly from above, a sharp whistle sounds shrilly. The blind man stops for a second as though perplexed. Again the whistle sounds.

EXTERIOR MARGIE'S HOUSE—SHOOTING THROUGH WINDOW
Nick's face is pressed against the bars. Again he whistles with his fingers.

LONG SHOT—WATERFRONT—FROM NICK'S ANGLE
The beggar is tapping his way down the street, oblivious to the whistle.

INTERIOR MARGIE'S ROOM

CLOSE SHOT—NICK AT WINDOW
He looks down the street hopelessly. He is about to whistle again when:

MARGIE'S VOICE: *(ironically)* Aren't you afraid someone might hear you?

Nick turns. Camera draws back, revealing Margie in the room. She is carrying a tray on which are tea and breakfast. In the open door we can see a Chinese guard, gun in hand. Itzumi stands behind the guard, fanning himself. Margie signals the two men. They leave.

MARGIE: *(setting down the tray)* I thought you might like some breakfast.

NICK: I'd like a few answers first.

Margie does not answer. Instead she pours tea.

NICK: *(continued)* How do I get out of here without being slugged again?

Margie does not answer.

NICK: *(continued)* You remind me of a dame in Egypt.

MARGIE: One of your ex-girl friends?

NICK: No—she was made of stone.

MARGIE: Oh—the Sphinx. Sometimes I wish I were made of stone.

NICK: *(studying her)* Wouldn't take much to prove you're not.

He takes her hand.

MARGIE: It never has.

She pulls her hand away. Nick smiles as we . . .

DISSOLVE

INTERIOR LOBBY HOTEL PORTUGUEZA—DAY
The clerk is at his desk as Julie comes downstairs.
CLERK: Good morning, senhora. Did you sleep well?
JULIE: Who slept? Has Mr. Cochran returned yet?
CLERK: No, senhora.
Julie exits.

EXTERIOR HOTEL PORTUGUEZA
As Julie comes out and signals for a ricksha driver. The blind beggar, Kwan Sum Tang, stands by the gate in an attitude of alertness. A ricksha comes up.
JULIE: The Quick Reward.
KWAN: *(recognizing Julie's voice)* Young lady.
JULIE: *(turning at ricksha)* Yes?
The beggar walks to the ricksha.
KWAN: You are a friend of the young American?
JULIE: *(surprised)* I was. Why?
KWAN: I know where he is.
JULIE: So what?
KWAN: He is in trouble.
JULIE: *(hesitates; then)* Get in.
KWAN: Only way I know is blind way. Follow me.
Kwan begins to walk slowly, Julie beside him.

DISSOLVE

A STREET IN MACAO—DAY
As Julie and Kwan walk. The blind man's pace is slow. The Chinese passersby look at the strange team with incredulity. Julie reacts as she spots an approaching car offstage. She quickly pulls the beggar into a doorway. A moment later, Sebastian's car passes, en route to the waterfront. Then once more they start their journey.

DISSOLVE

64

SECTION OF WATERFRONT—(PROCESS)

A fisherman mending his nets looks up as Sebastian hurries into scene.

SEBASTIAN: What boat did you rent last night?

FISHERMAN: No boat go out last night. Only one boat go—daytime.

SEBASTIAN: Who took it out?

FISHERMAN: *(calmly)* Man—American—Trumble. *(pointing to Chinese boy standing neaby)* Boy go out with him—catchee fish.

SEBASTIAN: *(turning to boy)* What did he do?

BOY: *(calmly)* Catchee fish.

SEBASTIAN: *(whirling on the fisherman)* Look—words go—Macao to Hong Kong—last night. No cable—no telephone. How talkee last night? Maybe boat?

FISHERMAN: *(beginning to mend a net)* Words can go without boat. Birds carry words. *(point to to clouds)* Devils in air make words . . . *(tapping on wood to simulate code)* White devils tap-tap-tap-tap—

Sebastian's face brightens as an idea strikes him.

SEBASTIAN: *(slowly—almost to himself)* Tap—tap . . .

THE WATERFRONT

As Julie and the blind man approach Margie's house.

JULIE: Are we there?

The blind man stops as a dog might do catching a scent.

JULIE: *(continued)* Which house is it?

Kwan does not answer. He moves with assurance, tapping his way along until he gets to a door. He stands motionlessly, then shakes his head. He moves to the next door, then stands the same way.

KWAN: *(finally)* This is the house.

Julie knocks. The door opens and Margie appears in the doorway.

MARGIE: Hello.

JULIE: Hello. You the lady of the house?

MARGIE: What's your mind?

JULIE: I heard you were taking in boarders. *Men* boarders.

MARGIE: Really?

JULIE: In all the heavy traffic, can you remember a guy called Nick?

MARGIE: What makes you think he's here?

JULIE: Let's ask him and find out.

MARGIE: Let's not.
JULIE: Why don't I look *now* and apologize *later?*
She shoves Margie aside and goes in.

INTERIOR MARGIE'S ROOM
Nick, who has been pacing, hears Julie's and Margie's voices.
JULIE'S VOICE: *(calling out)* Nick! It's me—Julie!
Nick reacts.

LOWER FLOOR
Margie stands by as Julie inspects the place.
JULIE: Nick! Nick, where are you?
She opens a door, looks in, then turns to go toward the stairs.
NICK'S VOICE: *(harshly)* What's the idea of horning in where you're
not wanted?
Julie looks up.

TOP OF STAIRCASE
We see Nick looking down.
NICK: Ever hear of the word privacy?

SECOND-FLOOR LANDING
*Now we see the reason for Nick's attitude. The Chinese guard is
covering the stairs with a drawn gun. He is so concealed that he
cannot be seen by Julie. Itzumi stands close by.*
NICK: Go back and chirp for Halloran—and keep out of my affairs.

JULIE AND MARGIE—(SHOT)
Julie reacts to Nick's harsh rejection of her. Margie smiles.
JULIE: *(finding words)* I just wanted to know if you were all right.

NICK—(SHOT)
NICK: *(insinuatively)* Why don't you ask Margie?

JULIE AND MARGIE—(SHOT)
MARGIE: He was afraid to go home in the fog—and my guest room
was handy.

66

NICK'S VOICE: You left out a few details, honey.

JULIE—(SHOT)
Obviously deeply hurt. She turns and goes out as Margie smiles.

SECOND-FLOOR LANDING—(SHOT)
Nick reacts to what has happened. Itzumi taps Nick with his fan to go back in the room. Nick obeys.

EXTERIOR MARGIE'S HOUSE—(TO BE SHOT)
As Julie stands weakly against the door, trying to collect her senses. Kwan Sum Tang moves up to her.
KWAN: You find him?
JULIE: *(dully)* Yes. Yes, I found him. Thanks.
She starts away.

EXTERIOR STREET DAY (PROCESS)
Of Julie as she walks, her face mirroring her disappointment.

DISSOLVE

CLOSE SHOT—SENHOR GARCIA
He is a handsome, tall, white-haired man in his sixties, an aristocrat to his fingertips. He is in the act of judging the flavor of a cigar held between his thin, beautifully chiseled lips. He takes a long puff and meditates.
GARCIA: *(speaking in cultured English with a Portuguese accent)* An excellent cigar.
Camera draws back to reveal that this is an elaborately furnished office situated on the second floor of one of Macao's larger buildings. Through the window in back of Garcia's desk may be seen the harbor.
Trumble stands beside Garcia, his salesman's kit open on a table.
TRUMBLE: I wish you could visit our Sumatra plantation, Senhor Garcia. We grow the finest tobacco leaf in the world.
GARCIA: *(with a smile)* It is pleasant to do business with you, senhor. My firm can use five hundred boxes.

67

TRUMBLE: I knew you were a man who'd recognize value.

Garcia brings forth two wine glasses and a decanter.

GARCIA: Allow me to offer you some Madeira. *(as he pours)* For three centuries these grapes have been grown by my family in Portugal. *(sighing)* Sometimes, I think it's a pity that the world cannot mellow like this wine.

He offers a glass to Trumble. At this moment the door opens and Sebastian enters with Halloran.

GARCIA: *(continued) (coolly)* Lieutenant Sebastian—Senhor Halloran—

SEBASTIAN: I regret the interruption, Senhor Garcia, but the hotel clerk informed us that Senhor Trumble would be here. There are several questions I should like to ask.

TRUMBLE: *(laughing—to Halloran)* Don't tell me my check bounced already.

SEBASTIAN: I should like to know your whereabouts last night, Senhor Trumble.

TRUMBLE: Around what time?

SEBASTIAN: I must warn you, senhor, that the clerk at the hotel informs me you left at eleven-thirty and did not return.

GARCIA: *(interrupting)* Mr. Trumble was our guest last night.

HALLORAN: And never went out?

GARCIA: Are you on the police force now, Mr. Halloran?

SEBASTIAN: Someone was so bold as to board Senhor Halloran's boat last night—and break open his shortwave set.

GARCIA: Senhor Trumble could hardly be your culprit. He stayed at our home all night.

SEBASTIAN: I presume that your wife would verify this.

GARCIA: By all means. I will call her. *(lifting phone)* Call my home, please.

TRUMBLE: What's all the excitement about a wireless set—did they steal it?

GARCIA: *(continued) (into phone—in Portuguese—affectionately)* Margharita? . . . I am sorry to disturb you, my dear one, but Lieutenant Sebastan wishes to ask you some questions about Senhor Trumble. *(meaningfully)* He wishes to verify that Senhor Trumble was our guest all last night.

He hands the phone to Sebastian.
SEBASTIAN: *(at phone—in Portuguese)* Senhora—it is a pleasure to hear your voice. How are you feeling . . . very well, thank you . . . I am sorry to disturb you, but I wish to inquire whether you had a houseguest last night.
> *Everyone is looking at Sebastian. It is obvious from the expression on Sebastian's face that Senhora Garcia has confirmed her husband's words.*
SEBASTIAN: *(continued) (into phone)* I see . . . thank you. I am sorry to have caused you an inconvenience.
> *Sebastian hangs up as Halloran reacts to this new proof of Trumble's innocence.*
HALLORAN: *(angrily to Sebastian)* You and your brilliant ideas! *(to others)* Sorry, gentlemen.
SEBASTIAN: My regrets, senhors.
TRUMBLE: Forget it. *(offering one)* Have a cigar.
> *Garcia bows. Sebastian and Halloran leave. There is a long pause as Trumble looks at Garcia.*
GARCIA: *(picking up his glass)* Someday our city will be free of men like that.
TRUMBLE: *(toasting with his wine)* Someday, senhor, I must meet that very wonderful wife of yours . . .

DISSOLVE

INTERIOR HALLORAN'S OFFICE—AFTERNOON
Halloran stands at the window, looking out. His assurance is slipping away from him. Sebastian moves restlessly.
HALLORAN: *(gesturing out the window)* I took this town and choked it with my bare hands until it coughed up.
SEBASTIAN: *(placatingly)* You have gone far.
HALLORAN: Far? *(desperately)* I can't go beyond the three-mile limit! I'm like a king shut up in his own castle! And even with Cochran under lock and key, I can't leave Macao until I know who's working with him. *(fearfully)* How did that diamond get away from my fence in Hong Kong? Who communicated with the American consul last night? *(his fear growing)* What kind of a spy system have you got?

69

SEBASTIAN: *(pompously)* It was I who discovered that someone had used the shortwave on your boat.

HALLORAN: *(sarcastically)* Congratulations. But who used it? Not Trumble. Not the girl. *(desperately)* We've got to make Cochran talk.

SEBASTIAN: I beg you—nothing must happen to the American. My job is at stake.

HALLORAN: *(grimly)* My life is at stake.

SEBASTIAN: *(with a sadistic smile)* If it were anyone else, I'd say you were frightened.

HALLORAN: I'll show you how frightened I am. I'm going to Hong Kong tonight. I'll find out how that stone got back here.

SEBASTIAN: But will you find out who has been working with him here?

HALLORAN: *(as an idea strikes him)* Yes—I'll even know that—and before I sail tonight.

As Sebastian looks at him, puzzled, camera moves in on the small wooden god as we . . .

DISSOLVE

CLOSE SHOT—HUGE STONE CHINESE GOD—NIGHT

It is an immense replica of the small figurine on Halloran's desk.

MERCHANT'S VOICE: He is the god in charge of the Ninth Section of Hell.

Camera draws back and we are in a curio shop surrounded by hundreds of Chinese gods in ivory, plaster, terra cotta—all sitting on the shelves. Trumble is standing with the proprietor looking at the god of power.

TRUMBLE: What's his job?

At this moment Kwan Sum Tang taps his way into the shop.

MERCHANT: He repays in violence all those who are violent.

TRUMBLE: He must be a busy man. Can you wrap up those ash trays for me?

As the merchant disappears behind the counter, Kwan Sum Tang and Trumble move casually to a corner. We do not know what they are saying. Camera pans to the image of a tremendous Chinese god. It is the god of ferocity, and its face symbolizes this.

70

Camera holds on the Chinese god. The image blurs and dissolves to a close shot of a shallow puddle. In the puddle can be seen the reflection of the face of Itzumi.
Camera moves up from puddle—discloses Itzumi pressed into the shadow of a doorway, across the street from Margie's house.

DISSOLVE

INTERIOR MARGIE'S ROOM—NIGHT
Nick lies on the bed. He is fully clothed, his shirt open at the neck. Suddenly an eerie, creaky sound is heard. He turns. To his amazement, the door of his room opens slowly. Nick walks to the doorway, peers out into the hall. He reacts to the quiet, goes out into the hall.

SECOND-FLOOR LANDING
As Nick comes out. The landing is empty. Nick reacts. He begins to walk stealthily down the stairs.

LOWER FLOOR—MARGIE'S HOUSE
Nick comes down the stairs. He moves carefully to the front door, tries the knob. To his surprise, the door swings open.
MARGIE'S VOICE: Don't go out there.
Nick turns quickly.

MARGIE
Now we see her lying on a divan in the shadows. She is listening to a Chinese record—singsong, dreamy music. Nick walks over to her.
MARGIE: *(with a strange smile)* Stay here and you'll be safe.
NICK: For how long?
MARGIE: *(dreamily)* Does it matter?
Nick looks at Margie, then at the door. He smiles wryly, pats her on the arm.
NICK: Sorry, baby, I'll have to take a rain check.
He goes out.

71

EXTERIOR MARGIE'S HOUSE
As Nick comes out. For a moment he stands still, clearing his head. He begins to walk. Camera pans to reveal Itzumi still standing in the shadows, then moving after Nick a moment later.

A DESOLATE STREET
As Nick walks, determinedly. Suddenly he stops, looks back over his shoulder.

THE STREET FROM NICK'S ANGLE
It is empty.

NICK
He throws off his sudden sense of being followed, starts to walk again, faster this time. A metallic sound comes closer and closer to him. He tenses, stops. The sound grows louder. Then the sound stops close to him. He looks.

A TIN CAN
It has been kicked and rolled down the street. This is what has frightened him.

NICK
He is terrorized by his own fear. He hurries around a corner.

THE STREET
As Nick walks. We hear footsteps keeping time with his own.

NICK
He is listening, alerted. He is sure now of the footsteps behind him. He tries an experiment . . . takes one—two—three—four—five—six steps. Whoever is following keeps exact time with those footsteps. Quickly he backs into a doorway. He waits. There is no sound. He begins to breathe heavily. Fear is enveloping him. As he stands against the door, he hears a click. He looks down at the door handle, reacts. The door begins to open slowly. Then it closes again. Panic begins to grip Nick, and he runs out of the doorway.

72

STREET
As Nick begins to run along the empty street.

STREET CORNER
As Nick comes around the corner. He stops and presses against the wall.

LAMPPOST FROM NICK'S EYELINE
A man looking like Itzumi is standing under the lamppost.

NICK
As he waits breathlessly.

MAN
As he leaves the lamppost and begins to walk in Nick's direction.

NICK
As he darts away in the other direction. But he has not run twenty steps when he comes up sharp.

SECOND MAN FROM NICK'S EYELINE
He has appeared from nowhere.

NICK
He looks up at the door against which he leans. There is a light over the door. He runs in.

INTERIOR JOSS HOUSE
It is grimy and dim and filthy. Dim figures move in a haze. A sinister face looms up to Nick. Nick pushes past him.

LONG HALL
It is dark. Nick rushes through it until he reaches a door. He opens the door.

COURTYARD

It is fenced in. Nick looks around him. There is no way to get out except to climb the fence. Nick jumps high, pulls himself over the fence.

DISSOLVE

EXTERIOR ALLEY—NIGHT
As Nick runs. His head aches and he stops, putting his hand to his head. At this moment there is a screech and something black falls on Nick's shoulder. Nick brushes it off.

A CAT
As it runs across the street. Nick runs on.

DISSOLVE

INTERIOR CORRIDOR THIRD FLOOR HOTEL PORTU-GUEZA
As Nick hurries to Trumble's door.

OUTSIDE TRUMBLE'S DOOR
Nick tries the handle.

INTERIOR TRUMBLE'S ROOM
It is pitch black. Nick enters. He moves to the bed. He discovers that Trumble is not in the room. At this moment he hears footsteps down the hall. Quickly he steps out onto Trumble's balcony.

EXTERIOR SECOND-FLOOR BALCONY
As Nick comes climbing down from the third floor to the second-floor balcony. He opens Julie's balcony door.

INTERIOR JULIE'S ROOM
He comes through it, opens the door.

SECOND-FLOOR CORRIDOR

As Nick comes out of Julie's room, he hears the hotel clerk in the lobby, talking Cantonese.

LOBBY
Itzumi and two Chinese are talking to the desk clerk.

NICK
As he dashes up the stairs.

EXTERIOR ROOF OF HOTEL PORTUGUEZA—NIGHT
It is like a black billiard table bathed in moonlight. The tin door creaks open and Nick appears. He begins to walk across the roof. Suddenly there is a creaking sound. Nick wheels, as a Chinese with a knife rushes at Nick. Nick grabs the man's wrist. They begin to struggle. They get closer and closer to the edge of the roof. Nick gets a neck hold on the Chinese and pushes. As the man falls over the edge of the roof, we hear a deathly scream.

EXTERIOR WALL AND LADDER
As Nick climbs down the ladder. We see him leap to a lower roof. He runs along from one roof to another.

NICK
As he creeps to the edge of the parapet of the roof and looks down the street.

STREET
In the brightly lighted street below we see Itzumi in front of the hotel, looking up. Across the street is another man. At the corner a third.

EXTERIOR ROOFTOPS
As Nick races along the rooftops. Finally there are no more roofs—the only way he can get down is by grabbing a flagpole and swinging from the flagpole to an awning. Camera follows Nick as he takes his chance. The flagpole splinters. Nick falls. He lands on an awning—scrambles to safety.

DISSOLVE

ANOTHER ALLEY—NIGHT
It is something out of a nightmare—houses throw grotesque shadows on the cobblestones. Nick flees down the alley, comes to a fence, leaps over it.

WATERFRONT
The moon has gone behind a cloud. Nick comes running across the cobblestones. He hears something again. He hides behind a fishnet.

ITZUMI
As he stalks in and out of fishnets.

MOVING SHOT
As Nick hurries through nets, aware he is on the verge of being trapped. Suddenly he trips and something drapes itself over his head.

NICK
As he struggles out of the shroud. It is a large fishnet into which he has become tangled. Breathlessly, he looks around. Suddenly the footsteps are heard again. Nick hides in a dock, trying to get his breath. He looks around desperately.

SHACK FROM NICK'S EYELINE
It is made of bamboo slatting, one side open to the water.

NICK
As he makes a dash for the shack.

ITZUMI AND HENCHMEN
They creep stealthily toward the shack, ready for the kill.

INTERIOR SHACK

It is dark as Nick hurries in. Suddenly a hand comes out and touches him. Nick reels. Something flashes in the dark. It is Trumble's diamond ring. Now we see Trumble standing there, leaning against the bamboo wall on the waterfront side. Quickly he presses a gun into Nick's hand.

EXTERIOR SHACK
As Itzumi slowly draws out his fan. He extracts from its folds a slender, file-like knife. He aims, then plunges the knife into the bamboo wall of the shack.

INTERIOR SHACK
The bamboo wall seems to lurch. Trumble gives a lunge forward and a moan. Nick remains motionless.

EXTERIOR SHACK
As Itzumi withdraws the dagger, places it back into his fan. Behind him can now be seen his henchmen. He joins them.

INTERIOR SHACK
Trumble staggers away from Nick, clawing at his back where the dagger had struck. With a splash, Trumble falls into the water. Outside there is the sound of footsteps running away. Nick jumps into the water.

THE WATER
As Nick comes to Trumble and pulls him to dock.
TRUMBLE: *(with a smile of pain)* You're always pulling dead people out of the water—
NICK: Take it easy.
Trumble tries to talk. With his last dying strength he forces Nick to listen.
TRUMBLE: No good now—sorry—used you to try to get Halloran—out to the three-mile limit—police boat waiting there—thought you could help. It's all fixed for you to go home—if you want to. *(as he dies)* I'm going home, too—the shortest way.

NICK
As he reacts to Trumble's death.

DISSOLVE

EXTERIOR HALLORAN'S BOAT—NIGHT
As Itzumi climbs over the railing, starts for wheel. Suddenly he hears footsteps above. He crouches in the cabinway to hide from sight. Footsteps come closer. Itzumi peers up at the dock and his face relaxes.

AT DOCK
Margie appears, impassive and alluring. Itzumi comes over to her.
ITZUMI: What are you doing here?
MARGIE: Is the master leaving tonight?
ITZUMI: Yes—go away.
MARGIE: Is he not afraid of the American detective?
ITZUMI: No—he left Macao quite suddenly. *(with a smile)* Accidental drowning.
MARGIE: And his friend—did he lead you to them?
ITZUMI: He had none.
MARGIE: What about the girl who sings—is she not his friend?
ITZUMI: The master is taking her to Hong Kong tonight.
MARGIE: It is a nice night for a pleasant voyage.
At this moment a hand comes in and throttles Itzumi.

MARGIE
Reacting.

DISSOLVE

EXTERIOR HALLORAN PIER—NIGHT
As chauffeur-driven car pulls up to the dock. Halloran helps Julie out. They move toward the boat.
HALLORAN: Sixty minutes and we'll be in Hong Kong. Looking forward to it?

JULIE: Anything you say.
As they reach the boat, the pilot is already at the wheel, staring at the dark water. He blows the boat whistle.
HALLORAN: *(calling out)* Start your motors!
As Halloran helps Julie down into the boat . . .

DISSOLVE

CABIN OF BOAT—NIGHT (PROCESS)
Julie leans back, letting the spray shower her face.
HALLORAN: Glad you came?
JULIE: It's nice to get away from that sewer.
HALLORAN: *(exultantly pointing)* There's the three-mile limit. The emperor is out of his castle!
He looks ahead to the skipper.

BACK OF SKIPPER
His face is hidden. Everything seems in order.

SKIPPER
We now reveal it is Nick.

HALLORAN AND JULIE
He looks toward shore, slightly perplexed.
HALLORAN: He should be heading up the coast, instead of out to sea. *(gets up)* Be right back, honey.
He walks over to the skipper. Nick whirls around and leaps.

DIRECTOR'S SHOTS
Dramatizing the struggle between Halloran and Nick in the boat. As they slug it out, the boat lurches in the water and the salt spray flies. Nick orders to Julie to take the wheel. The fight continues, first to Nick's advantage, then Halloran's advantage, etc. . . . until Nick hurls Halloran in the water, then dives in, knocks him out with a punch as he comes up; suddenly a searchlight hits the two men.
STEWART'S VOICE: Ahoy there! Need any help?

79

Nick turns to look.

NICK: Could have used you five minutes ago.

EXTERIOR DECK OF INTERPOL BOAT—(PROCESS)
Stewart is revealed as boat pulls up slowly.
STEWART: I presume that's Halloran.

FULL SHOT
As the two boats close in. Julie is leaning over the rail anxiously.
NICK: What's left of him.
Halloran and Nick are pulled aboard.
STEWART: I'm Captain Stewart of the International Police Commission. Where's Lieutenant Bryan?
NICK: Bryan?
STEWART: I think you knew him as Trumble. Where is he?
NICK: *(soberly)* He didn't make it, Captain.
Stewart looks at him understandingly.
STEWART: Aren't you coming aboard?
NICK: No—I've got some unfinished business.
As he starts to swim back to Halloran's boat . . .

DISSOLVE

EXTERIOR MACAO DOCKS—DAY (STOCK)
Showing the most colorful part of the city.

EXTERIOR HARBOR—(STOCK)
Showing ferry far across the rooftops, as it sails up the river.

EXTERIOR COASTLINE—(STOCK)
As we see it pass from the ship.

DISSOLVE

INTERIOR SHIP BAR—DAY
Bartender is waiting on a man in civilian clothes.
BARTENDER: No more uniform, Lieutenant?

The man turns and we see that it is Sebastian.

SEBASTIAN: No more lieutenant.

BARTENDER: What happened?

SEBASTIAN: Politics. It seems I backed the wrong horse. *(turning to someone offstage)* Another drink, Adam?

Camera angle widens and we see Nick is also seated at the bar.

NICK: No, thanks. *(indicating deck window)* Can't keep Eve waiting.

Another angle—revealing Julie's legs pacing up deck as in early scene of picture. Nick gets up and leaves.

SEBASTIAN: *(sardonically, to bartender)* And so I bid farewell to beautiful Macao—always friendly and hospitable.

He downs his drink.

Closer shot—window, as Nick's legs move into scene. Julie stops pacing and they come closer together, evidently kissing, as we . . .

FADE OUT

THE END